TEACH READING
with **Orton-Gillingham:**
EARLY
READING
SKILLS

TEACH READING

with **Orton-Gillingham:**
EARLY READING SKILLS

A Companion Guide with Dictation Activities, Decodable Passages, and Other Supplemental Materials for Struggling Readers and Students with Dyslexia

Heather MacLeod-Vidal
& Kristina Smith

ULYSSES PRESS

Published by:
ULYSSES PRESS
PO Box 3440
Berkeley, CA 94703
www.ulyssespress.com

ISBN: 978-1-64604-405-4
Library of Congress Control Number: 2022936254

Printed in the United States by Kingery Printing Company
10 9 8 7 6 5 4 3 2 1

Acquisitions editor: Casie Vogel
Managing editor: Claire Chun
Editor: Renee Rutledge
Proofreader: Barbara Schultz
Front cover design and interior design/layout: what!design @ whatweb.com
Cover art: © BNP Design Studio/shutterstock.com
Interior art: from shutterstock.com
Production: Yesenia Garcia-Lopez

"To all of the children learning how to read, especially my own children, Juniper and Florence."
— Heather

"To my father, whose pride in and support of my first book inspired me to write this second book. Although you are now only able to support me in spirit, I thank and love you always."
— Kristina

CONTENTS

Unit 5: Vowel Teams 135

About the Authors 151

INTRODUCTION

Dear Educator,

This book was written to support teachers who are using a structured literacy approach within their classrooms or tutoring settings. It is written and aligned to match our lesson plan book, *Teach Reading with Orton-Gillingham*, but can be useful as a supplement for most phonics programs.

The activities in this book include Phonemic Awareness Warm-Up Drills, Letter Tile Word Building, Word Sorts, decodable text, and dictation of words and sentences. They can be used after following our correlated lesson plan in *Teach Reading with Orton-Gillingham*, or after explicit teaching of the skill noted within the lesson.

Every lesson follows a similar layout and structure. This predictability helps students master skills more readily because they are prepared for what is to come. All of the words, sentences, and passages are written to include only the phonics skills and sight words that have been previously taught. Tricky words, or sight words that are not yet decodable, are noted at the top of the passages to prepare students further for reading.

Each lesson will also include word building and sorts. These word-building activities provide a multisensory approach to make learning more engaging and effective.

Every component of this book was designed to help students learn to read in a way that is systematic, explicit, and fun!

Happy teaching!

Heather and Kristina

Decodable Text

How does decodable text fit into classroom use?

Explicit phonics instruction with decodable text is essential for early readers and is an important component of Orton-Gillingham–based instruction. This methodology allows students to use what they are learning in their phonics lessons and apply it to text. This type of reading encourages using phonics above all else to read. Decodable text can, and should, be used to support early readers. Decodable passages and books can be used as a means of instruction, assessment, small group work, and independent reading choices. They can also be sent home for parents to read with their children.

What does the research say?

Research supports the use of decodable texts for students who are still mastering the alphabetic principle.[1] Studies have concluded that explicit phonics instruction with the use of decodable text increases students' abilities to read in comparison to students who use non-controlled leveled readers.[2] In one study, students who were identified as at-risk (below the fortieth percentile in reading) were randomly assigned to one of two basal readers. One group was given a highly decodable basal while the other was given a basal that relied more on context and pictures. The group of children who were assigned the "Code" basal that relied on more decodable text performed better on decoding and spelling tests at the end of their first-grade year than the "Context" basal. At the end of both groups' second-grade year, the students in the "Code" group performed better on both the decoding measure and the reading of real, regular, multisyllabic words.[3]

Is there still a place for leveled readers?

Decodable readers should be utilized for students who are still learning "the code." Once students have mastered most phonics skills, leveled readers are a great way to encourage and support readers. Leveled readers are also an excellent choice for read-alouds to encourage listening comprehension and targeted comprehension practice.

Phonological and Phonemic Awareness

What is phonological and phonemic awareness?

Phonological awareness is the ability to hear and manipulate the parts of words. Skills such as rhyming, breaking words into syllables, and identifying onset and rime are all part of phonological awareness. Phonemic awareness is the narrowed focus of identifying individual sounds within words. For example, in the word ship, there are three sounds, /sh/, /i/, and /p/.

Why should I teach phonological and phonemic awareness?

Phonological awareness is an essential skill for students. Learning to "map" sounds helps build the bridge students need to connect oral language to written words.[4] According to David Kilpatrick, one of the leading researchers in phonological and phonemic awareness, "Students with good phonological awareness are in a great position to become good readers, while students with poor phonological awareness almost always struggle in reading."[5]

How is phonological and phonemic awareness broken down in this book?

Each lesson in this book will begin with a quick phonological and/or phonemic awareness warm-up lasting two to four minutes. These lessons may not always align with the sounds being taught because these phonemic

1   K. Brown, "What Kind of Text: For Whom and When? Textual Scaffolding for Beginning Readers," *The Reading Teacher* 53, no. 4 (1999): 292–307; H. A. Mesmer, "Scaffolding a Crucial Transition Using Text with Some Decodability," *The Reading Teacher* 53, no. 2: (1999): 130–42.

2   C. Juel and D. Roper-Schneider, "The Influence of Basal Readers on First Grade Reading," *Reading Research Quarterly* 20, no. 2 (1985): 134–52.

3   R. H. Felton, "Effects of Instruction on the Decoding Skills of Children with Phonological Processing Problems," *Journal of Learning Disabilities*, 26, no. 9 (1993): 583–89.

4   D. Kilpatrick, *Essentials of Assessing, Preventing, and Overcoming Reading Difficulties* (Boston: John Wiley and Sons, 2015).

5   D. Kilpatrick, *Equipped for Reading Success: A Comprehensive, Step-by-Step Program for Developing Phonemic Awareness and Fluent Word Recognition* (Syracuse, New York: Casey & Kirsch Publishers, 2016).

awareness activities are designed to be done orally and auditorily. With that said, there is strong research that suggests linking letters to sounds is a powerful tool during phonemic awareness activities. We suggest pointing out sounds by stating their letter names if and when you think your students are ready.

Unit 1 will focus on phonological awareness by identifying initial, final, and medial sounds.

Units 2 to 5 will focus on phonological and phonemic awareness by blending, segmenting, and manipulating phonemes.

What is the recommended scope and sequence of phonological and phonemic awareness instruction?

Students will begin by identifying the initial, final, and medial sounds of words, and will end the book with more complex phoneme substitution and manipulation. The phonological/phonemic awareness drill, or PA Warm-Up, will always be scripted.

Here are some examples of prompts and activities you will see throughout this book. The drills will become more complex as the book progresses.

- **Identifying Initial Sounds:** Say the words on the list. Have students tell you the first sound of each word. Example: dog (/d/)
- **Identifying Final Sounds:** Say the words on the list. Have students tell you the final sound of each word. Example: pat (/t/)
- **Identifying Medial Sounds:** Say the words on the list. Have students tell you the medial (vowel) sound of each word. Example: kit (/i/)
- **Identifying Targeted Sounds:** Say the words on the list. Have students tell you if they hear a /sh/ (like in ship), or a /zsh/ like in beige.
- **Identifying Parts of Words:** Say the following plural words. Have students tell you the base word of each word. Example: puffs (puff)
- **Phoneme Blending:** Separate all of the sounds in the words on the list. Then have students tell you the whole word. Example: /n/ /u/ /t/ (nut)
- **Phoneme Segmentation:** Say the words on the list. Have students tell you the sounds in each word. Example: make (/m/ /ā/ /k/)
- **Phoneme Deletion of Initial Sounds:** Say the words on the list. Have students tell each word without the initial sound. Example: fun (un)
- **Phoneme Deletion of Final Sounds:** Say the words on the list. Have students say each word without the final sound. Example: finch (fin)
- **Phoneme Substitution:** Say the word on the list, but have students change one sound with a different letter. Examples: Replace the first sound in chick with /k/ (kick) or replace the vowel sound /ā/ in take with /ĭ/ (tick).

It is important to note that the letters represented for these activities are often different from the spelling of a word. For instance, the hard *c*, *k*, and *-ck* will all be represented by /k/ since that is the phonetic spelling for that sound. Long vowels are represented by a single letter with a macron (ā) and short vowels are represented by a single letter with a breve (ă). Silent letters will not be represented since only sounds are used for these activities.

Word Work

Where can I find the letter tiles in color?

Our free letter tiles can be found by visiting our website, www.treetopseducation.com/teach-reading. Tiles in black and white are located on "Letter Tiles" on page 150. We suggest printing two copies and coloring the vowels (rows 1 and 2) red, the consonants and consonant digraphs (rows 3 to 6) yellow, and the glued sounds (rows 7 and 8) green, then laminating and cutting.

How should I use letter tiles with this book?

Letter/sound tiles are used during every lesson to build and manipulate words using the targeted sounds from the lesson. Instruct the students to start with the initial word. Then go through the list in order by instructing students to build each word with their letter tiles. Students will change one or two tiles at a time (with the exception of a few lessons where they will change all of the letters to change the syllable). Many sorts have recommended vocabulary words to review during the word-chaining activities.

What are the symbols in the Word Work section?

Nonsense words appear frequently throughout Word Work and dictation. You will notice that nonsense words are always marked with a star. Words that require more than one tile change are underlined.

What are some activities I can do with the Word Sorts?

Exploration: We recommend starting every Word Sort with an exploration. Have your student cut out the words and think about the ways that the words could be sorted. They may surprise you with their ideas.

Teach and Sort: This should be included with every sort. This is a good time to teach your students how the words should be sorted using the included headers. You may choose to point out commonalities in words that will help your students identify how to sort the words.

Speed Sort: Practice timing your students. After one sort, have your student set a timed goal for the next sort. Can they beat their time?

Partner Sort: One person reads the word, the other decides what category the word should go under.

Written Sort: The teacher reads the words, the student writes it on a whiteboard under the category with which it belongs.

Picture Sort: The student picks words to write and illustrate.

What are the vocabulary practice words listed in some lessons?

These are words that may be unfamiliar to your students. We recommend reviewing the definitions of these words during the Word Sort activity.

Why are there blank spots on every Word Sort?

We encourage students to come up with their own word additions in every sort. If they cannot come up with new words, invite them to use any from the lesson.

What should I do when my student has practiced several sort activities?

We suggest having your students glue the words into a notebook under the correct categories.

Dictation

What can I do to make spelling and dictation more successful for my students?

Finger tapping is a great way to help students spell words. Tapping helps build the idea that sounds and graphemes are connected. This multisensory method is easy to implement and essential within the Orton-Gillingham approach. Students need to understand that letters have their own sounds, but they slide into the next sound without pause. Teach students to tap on the hand they do not write with so they can practice tapping as they write.

To be clear, finger tapping is more about associating sounds with letters, so tapping will not include silent letters. For words with more than five sounds, students can start again from their first finger.

Finger-Tapping Rules:

1. Tap once for each sound.

2. Digraphs get one tap only (*th, sh, wh, ch*, etc.).

3. Vowel teams get one tap only (*ea, ee, oa, ai, igh*, etc.).

4. Glued sounds are tapped once with as many fingers as there are letters in the sound

(for example, *-ild* is tapped once with three fingers together).

5. Silent letters are not tapped; just sounds that are heard.

What are Elkonin boxes?

Elkonin boxes will be included on most of the dictation sheets in this book. This graphic tool is a useful way to connect correct spelling with finger tapping. The boxes teach students to segment words into their phonological parts. Each box represents a sound, but boxes can contain more than one letter if a consonant digraph, vowel team, or glued sound is in the word. Some pages do not include Elkonin boxes. This is because some patterns do not lend themselves as well to this strategy. On those pages, there are more lines for word writing.

What are the symbols on some of the dictation pages?

We use symbols on our dictation pages to scaffold students' spelling. Here are the symbols you may see on dictation pages. Many of these symbols will be phased out starting in Unit 3 as students become more proficient spellers.

Consonant Digraph:　⌣

Consonant Trigraph:　⌣—or—⌣

Glued Sound:　＿ ＿ ＿
　　　　　　　　　GS

Silent *e*:　☆

Vowel Team:　＿ ＿
　　　　　　　　VT

Some teachers also use symbols to designate capital letters and punctuation. You may want to add these to the dictation pages if this is something you want your students to work on.

In addition, as with the Word Work section, nonsense words are starred.

Sight Words

Many words that teachers previously taught as sight words (or "tricky words") are actually decodable. For example, the word "and" is not decodable when it is introduced in Unit 1, but after students have learned the nasal sound /an/ in Unit 2, it becomes decodable.

Here is the list of tricky words that are covered throughout the book. The words are organized by the unit in which they first appear. The words noted are not yet decodable at the time that they are introduced, but most will become decodable as students learn more spelling patterns.

Unit 1		Unit 2	Unit 3	Unit 4	Unit 5
and	to	what	each	could	place
the	she	from	made	into	year
be	he	who	were	other	me
look	was	her	find	word	very
said	one	an	now	write	after
you	two	for	some	their	our
can	like	your	way	water	good
go	see	are	part	number	sentence
I	them	use	they	people	great
so	first	there	time	over	where
do	come	been	would	new	
we	this	many	about	sound	
by	have		oil	only	
a	make		these	little	
no	down			work	
at	how			know	
but	or				
all	may				
of	than				
is	out				
day	more				
my					

Unit 1: Consonants, Consonant Digraphs, and Short Vowels

Unvoiced and Voiced Pairs

This curriculum teaches unvoiced and voiced pairs together. This means that the mouth and tongue make the same movement for each letter in a pair, but one sound uses air, and the other uses sound. Try looking in a mirror and putting your hand on your throat while you alternate between the unvoiced/voiced pairs below. You should see that your mouth makes the same movement for each.

Unvoiced	Voiced
p	*b*
t	*d*
k	*g*
f	*v*
s	*z*
ch	*j*
soft *th*	hard *th*

Spelling Rules Covered in This Unit

c/k: Hard *c* is used before consonants and the vowels *a*, *o*, and *u*. *K* is used before *e* and *i*.

Exceptions: Words such as koala, kangaroo, Korea, skate, kung fu, and skull.

k/-ck, c: *-ck* is used at the end of a one-syllable word right after a short vowel. Use *-k* in all other instances. The ending *-c*, or more specifically *-ic*, goes at the end of a two-syllable word ending in the /k/ sound.

Exceptions: When a suffix begins with *e, i,* or *y,* add a *k* after the *c* as in mimicked or panicking.

The Doubling Rule: If a word ends with a short vowel followed by *f, l, s,* or *z*, double it!

Exceptions:

- shortened words (bus, short for omnibus; gas, short for gasoline)
- words with long vowels (gross, troll)
- glued sounds (ball)
- endings with /z/ sound (his, was, is, has)
- yes, this, plus

Plural Spelling Rules: If a word ends with *-sh, -ch, x, s, z,* or a consonant plus *o*, add *-es*. If a word ends in *f*, change it to *v* and add *-es*. For all other words, add *-s*. When a word ends in *-s*, the *s* may sound like /s/ or /z/.

Exceptions: This rule does not apply to irregular nouns such as mouse (mice), tooth (teeth), foot (feet), man (men), fish, sheep, or deer.

Which new, and not yet decodable, sight words will be used in this unit's activities?

and	at	them
the	but	first
be	all	come
look	of	this
said	is	have
you	day	make
can	my	down
go	to	how
I	she	or
so	he	may
do	was	than
we	one	out
by	two	more
a	like	
no	see	

What are the symbols used on the dictation pages?

In order to provide scaffolds for early readers and writers, we provide symbols on the dictation pages to remind students to utilize patterns.

This is the symbol you will see throughout Unit 1: Consonant digraph (⌣)

What other information should I know?

Once vowels are introduced, students will begin dictation practice. We recommend having your student(s) read the decodable passage before the dictation practice. Also, in some lessons, the Word Sort activity is below the dictation page. We suggest cutting off that section before completing the dictation practice, as some of the words are duplicated.

Lesson 1 | Consonants *p* & *b*

Tips, Tricks, and Details

- The first three lessons of this book are shorter since there is no word reading until the first vowel is introduced. We recommend putting in the time to ensure students recognize these letters and sounds with strong automaticity.

- For some sounds, especially those for *b, c, d, g, p, t, k,* and *j,* it is very important to "clip" the letter sounds as you teach them. This means you must say the sound without adding a schwa /uh/ to the end of them. See *Teach Reading with Orton-Gillingham* or our website (www.treetopseducation.com/teach-reading) for more information on correct letter pronunciation.

PA Warm-Up

Identifying Initial Sounds

Say the words on the list below. Have students tell you the first sound of each word they hear. Example: pink (/p/)

pig (/p/)	pull (/p/)	bam (/b/)
bet (/b/)	pet (/p/)	pick (/p/)
pot (/p/)	putt (/p/)	ball (/b/)
bat (/b/)	bill (/b/)	page (/p/)

Initial Sound Sorting

Have students sort the following pictures under the appropriate initial sound. Encourage students to draw pictures in the remaining blanks with more *p* and *b* words.

pig	pencil	bone
pillows	penguin	bicycle
pear	pen	bee
pancakes	banana	backpack
pizza	bathtub	boots
panda	balloons	boat
pufferfish	ball	

Name: _____ Date: _____

Consonants *p* & *b*

Cut out the pictures. Then sort them under the appropriate header.

p	**b**		

	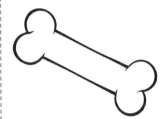		

TEACH READING with **Orton-Gillingham** EARLY READING SKILLS

Lesson 2 | Consonants *t* & *d*

PA Warm-Up

Identifying Initial Sounds

Say the words on the list below. Have students tell you the first sound of each word they hear. Example: dog (/d/)

top (/t/)	pass (/p/)	doll (/d/)
deal (/d/)	bug (/b/)	tail (/t/)
tack (/t/)	bed (/b/)	toss (/t/)
dill (/d/)	ding (/d/)	dip (/d/)

Initial Sound Sorting

Have students sort the following pictures under the appropriate initial sound. Encourage students to draw pictures in the remaining blanks with more *t* and *d* words.

tie	toaster	doctor
tooth	tea	dice
tent	dog	dinosaur
turtle	donut	doll
tiger	duck	door
taco	deer	
tape	dolphin	

Name: _____   Date: _____

Consonants *t* & *d*

Cut out the pictures. Then sort them under the **appropriate header**.

t	*d*		

	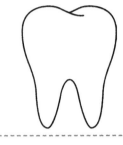		
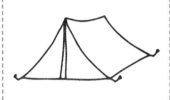	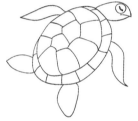		

Lesson 3 | Consonants *k & g*

Tips, Tricks, and Details

- At this point, the goal is to get students to identify the /k/ sound, not the different spellings of /k/. They will cover this during their first spelling rule lesson, *c*, *k*, and *-ck*.

- The letter *g* can also make a soft sound (like *c*) when it is followed by an *e*, *i*, or *y*. This concept is covered in Unit 7 in *Teach Reading with Orton-Gillingham*.

PA Warm-Up

Identifying Initial Sounds

Say the words on the list below. Have students tell you the first sound of each word they hear. Example: kite (/k/)

gum (/g/)	catch (/k/)	dim (/d/)
gills (/g/)	kiss (/k/)	bin (/b/)
kit (/k/)	gone (/g/)	pan (/p/)
kept (/k/)	tuck (/t/)	got (/g/)

Initial Sound Sorting

Have students sort the following pictures under the appropriate initial sound. Encourage students to draw pictures in the remaining blanks with more *k* and *g* words.

keys	kiss	gift
koala	kiwi	guitar
kangaroo	gumballs	gorilla
kick	glass	grandma
kitchen	ghost	grasshopper
king	grapes	goat
kettle	glasses	

Consonants *k & g*

Cut out the pictures. Then sort them under the appropriate header.

k	**g**		
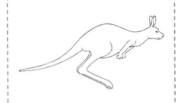			

Lesson 4 | Short *i*

Tips, Tricks, and Details

- During this lesson, students will be introduced to the first vowel sound taught in this unit. They will also begin blending two- and three-letter words, some of which are nonsense words.

- We recommend teaching initial blending using the continuous blending technique. This means that rather than stopping after each sound, you encourage students to stretch their sounds from one phoneme to the next. Please see our website, www.treetopseducation.com/teach-reading, for a video demonstrating this technique.

PA Warm-Up

Identifying Initial Sounds

Say the words on the list below. Have students tell you the first sound of each word they hear. Example: itch (/ĭ/)

ill (/ĭ/)	dim (/d/)	inch (/ĭ/)
kit(/k/)	igloo (/ĭ/)	ick (/ĭ/)
gill (/g/)	bill (/b/)	kiss (/k/)
tick (/t/)	pit (/p/)	kid (/k/)

Word Work

Instruct the students to begin with the start word. Then go through the list in order by instructing students to build each word with their letter tiles. Students will change one or two tiles at a time. Refer to page 150 for our letter tiles; for tiles in color, visit our website (www.treetopseducation.com/teach-reading). Nonsense words will be marked with a star, and words that require two tile changes will be underlined.

You will need the following letter tiles for this Word Work activity: *i, t, d, b, p, k, g*

Start word: it

Word list: bit, kit, pit, pig, ig*, dig, big, bip*, ip*, tip, dip

Dictation

> Write the following words in Elkonin boxes. Remember that each sound receives its own box.

1. bid

2. pit

3. dib

4. pig

> Write the following words on the word lines.

1. dig

2. kid

3. kit

> Write the following sentences on the sentence lines.

1. Go pig!

2. I dig.

Short *i*: Decodable

Read the story and draw a scene from it in the box.

Tricky Words: look, I, can, said, go, the, you, and

Pig and the Big Kid

"Look! I can dig!" said Pig.

"Go, Pig, go! Dig the big pit!" said the big kid.

"Can you dig?" said Pig.

"I can!" said the big kid.

The big kid and Pig can dig the big pit!

Word Sort

Cut out the words and pictures. Then sort them under the appropriate header.

Initial /ĭ/	Medial /ĭ/	it	bid	tip
dip	kit	bit		

Name: _____ Date: _____

Short *i*: Dictation

Elkonin Boxes

1.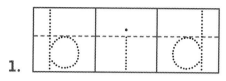

2.

3.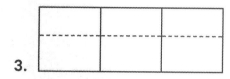

4.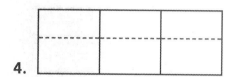

Words   Score: /3 words

1. _____

2. _____

3. _____

Sentences   Score: /4 words

1. _____

2. _____

Lesson 5 | Consonants *f* & *v*

Tips, Tricks, and Details

- During this lesson, students will be introduced to /f/. This sound can be represented by *f*, *ff*, *ph*, and *gh*. They will learn spelling patterns for *f* and *ff* in this unit, but the other patterns are not included until later in our *Teach Reading with Orton-Gillingham* sequence.

- Several nonsense words are used throughout this lesson. As a reminder, all nonsense words are starred.

PA Warm-Up

Identifying Initial Sounds

Say the words on the list below. Have students tell you the first sound of each word they hear. Example: fill (/f/)

fun (/f/)	fill (/f/)	ill (/ĭ/)
vet (/v/)	very (/v/)	got (/g/)
video (/v/)	Val (/v/)	kick (/k/)
fin (/f/)	for (/f/)	tell (/t/)

Word Work

You will need the following letter tiles for this Word Work activity: *i, f, v, t, d, b, p, k, g*

Start word: if

Word list: it, vit*, vid, fid*, fig, vig*, dig, big, bid, kid, kip, kit

Dictation

Write the following words in Elkonin boxes.

1. fin   **3.** if

2. vid   **4.** vip*

Write the following words on the word lines.

1. fip*   **3.** fit

2. vib*

Write the following sentences on the sentence lines.

1. Fit the kit.   **2.** Vib can dig.

Consonants *f* & *v*: Decodable

Read the story and fill in the blanks.

Tricky Words: look, the, said, I, can, you, we, and

The Big Fig

"Look, Pig! The big fig!" said the kid.

The kid bit the big fig.

"Look! I bit the big fig! Can you?" said the kid.

Pig bit the fig.

"I bit the fig!" said Pig.

"We bit the fig!" said Pig and the kid.

Comprehension

1. The kid bit the _____

2. The _____ and _____ bit the fig.

Consonants *f* & *v*: Dictation

Elkonin Boxes

1.

2.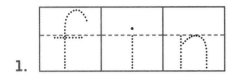

3.

4.

Words

Score: ___ /3 words

1. _____

2. _____

3. _____

Sentences

Score: ___ /6 words

1. _____

2. _____

Lesson 6 | Short *e*

Tips, Tricks, and Details

- This is the second vowel students will learn in this unit. Some students have a hard time differentiating between the short /ĭ/ sound and the short /ĕ/ sound. For these students, we recommend emphasizing the difference in mouth movement for each sound.

PA Warm-Up

Identifying Initial Sounds

Say the words on the list below. Have students tell you the first sound of each word they hear. Example: egg (/e/)

Ed (/ĕ/)	ten (/t/)	Ted (/t/)
end (/ĕ/)	pet (/p/)	fed (/f/)
elephant (/ĕ/)	best (/b/)	fell (/f/)
beg (/b/)	pen (/p/)	elk (/ĕ/)

Word Work

You will need the following letter tiles for this Word Work activity: *i, e, b, g, d, f, k, t*

Start word: beg

Word list: big, bid, bed, fed, fid*, fib, kib*, kid, kit, ket*

Dictation

Write the following words in Elkonin boxes.	
1. beg	**3.** fit
2. Ted	**4.** pig

Write the following words on the word lines.	
1. fed	**3.** dig
2. get	

Write the following sentences on the sentence lines.	
1. Ed did beg.	**2.** We get the peg.

Short *e*: Decodable

Read the story and underline the short *e* words.

Tricky Words: look, a, I, can, the, and, we, no

Ed, Peg, and Pig

"Look! A big bed! Can I get it?" Pig did beg.

Ed can get Pig the big bed.

"Look! A fig and dip! Can I get the fig and dip?" Pig did beg.

Peg fed Pig a fig and dip.

"Look! A vet! Can we get the vet?" Ed and Peg did beg.

"No! No vet!" Pig did beg.

Ed and Peg did get Pig the vet.

Word Sort

Cut out the words and pictures. Then sort them under the appropriate header.

Initial /ĕ/	Medial /ĕ/	Ed	beg	Ted
bet	Deb	pet		

Name: _____   Date: _____

Short *e*: Dictation

Elkonin Boxes

1.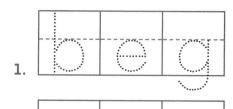

2.

3.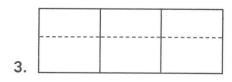

4.

Words   Score: /3 words

1. _____   2. _____   3. _____

Sentences   Score: /7 words

1.

2.

Lesson 7 | Consonants *s* & *z*

Tips, Tricks, and Details

- Savvy students may notice that *s* can sometimes make a /z/ sound, especially when it is positioned at the end of a word (has, rings, etc.). Words that end in a vowel or certain consonants (*b, d, g, l, m, n, ng, r, v*) have a "voiced" *s* sound, which sounds like /z/. Students will cover this more in the Plural Spelling Rule lesson on page 72.

- This lesson will cover *s* and *z* in the initial position. Final positions in short vowel words will be covered in the Doubling Rule lesson on page 70, and the Plural Spelling Rule lesson on page 72.

PA Warm-Up

Identifying Initial Sounds

Say the words on the list below. Have students tell you the first sound of each word they hear. Example: sit (/s/)

sight (/s/)	ebb (/ĕ/)	sing (/s/)
zip (/z/)	ill (/ĭ/)	zap (/z/)
sap (/s/)	fun (/f/)	city (/s/)
zing (/z/)	vet (/v/)	center (/s/)

Word Work

You will need the following letter tiles for this Word Work activity: *s, i, p, z, t, g, e*

Start word: sip

Word list: zip, zit, sit, sig*, zig, zeg*, seg*, set, zet*

Dictation

Write the following words in Elkonin boxes.

1. Zeb   **3.** sep*

2. seg*   **4.** zit

Write the following words on the word lines.

1. Sid   **3.** sib*

2. zip

Write the following sentences on the sentence lines.

1. Zed can get a fig.   **2.** The pig can sit and sip.

Name: _____ Date: _____

Consonants *s* & *z*: Decodable

Read and underline words that have an *s* or *z*.

Tricky Words: can, and, by, the, go

Zed and Bev

Zed is a pet pig. Zed can dig and Zed can sit.

Zed can zip by the kid, Bev. "Go, Zed, go!" said Bev.

Comprehension

Students may need help with the italicized words.

What can Zed do?

_____

_____

Word Sort

Cut out the words and pictures. Then sort them under the appropriate header.

s	**z**	sit	zit	set
zip	sip	zig		

Consonants *s* & *z*: Dictation

Elkonin Boxes

1.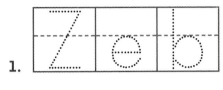

2.

3.

4.

Words   Score: /3 words

1. _____   2. _____   3. _____

Sentences   Score: /11 words

1. _____

2. _____

Lesson 8 | Short *a*

Tips, Tricks, and Details

- This lesson will cover short *a*, as in apple. *A* makes a nasal sound when positioned before an *m* or *n* (can, Sam). To demonstrate this, have your students plug their noses while saying the word *apple*. Then have them say the word *can*. They will notice that the sound comes from their nose. This will be covered more on page 89.

- The letter *a* can also sound different when placed before an *l* (ball, malt). This will be covered more on page 92.

PA Warm-Up

Identifying Initial Sounds

Say the words on the list below. Have students tell you the first sound of each word they hear. Example: add (/ă/)

it (/ĭ/)	sat (/s/)	apt (/ă/)
at (/ă/)	bad (/b/)	lap (/l/)
act (/ă/)	tack (/t/)	tap (/t/)
itch (/ĭ/)	ab (/ă/)	pat (/p/)

Word Work

You will need the following letter tiles for this Word Work activity: *a, i, e, b, t, d, p, s, z*

Start word: bet

Word list: bat, bit, bid, bed, bad, tad, tap, tip, sip, sap, zap

Note that several vocabulary words have been identified in this word chaining activity. We recommend defining these for students as you proceed through the activity.

Vocabulary practice: bid, tad, sap

Dictation

Write the following words in Elkonin boxes.

1. bad   **3.** vat

2. tag   **4.** big

Write the following words on the word lines.

1. tab   **3.** sap

2. fed

Write the following sentences on the sentence lines.

1. Get the bad bat!   **2.** Look at Pat zig and zag.

Short *a*: Decodable

Read and underline the short *a* words.

Tricky Words: the, a, by, and, can, you, said

Pat and Jed

Pat is a big bat. Jed is a kid bat. Jed sat by Pat. Pat and Jed gab and gab.

"Jed, can you get the sap?" said Pat.

"I can get the sap. Can you get a bag and a sap tap?" said Jed.

"I can!" said Pat. Pat did get the sap tap and bag.

Jed did get the sap. Pat and Jed sat and Pat fed Jed the sap.

Word Sort

Cut out the words and pictures. Then sort them under the appropriate header.

Initial /ă/	Medial /ă/	ab	fad	ad
at	sag	gab	fab	sad

Name: _____ Date: _____

Short *a*: Dictation

Elkonin Boxes

1.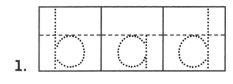

2.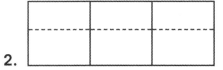

3.

4.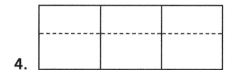

Words   Score: /3 words

1. _____   2. _____   3. _____

Sentences   Score: /10 words

1. _____

_____

2. _____

Lesson 9 | Consonants and Digraph *ch & j*

Tips, Tricks, and Details

- The sounds /ch/ and /j/ are an unvoiced/voiced pair which means the sounds are produced using the same mouth movement.

- *Ch* is a consonant digraph. Consonant digraphs are two letters that make one sound. For this particular digraph, the most common sound by far is the one made at the beginning of the word cheese. However, /ch/ can also make a /k/ sound, as in chaos, and a /sh/ sound, as in chef. This lesson will focus on the most common sound, /ch/ as in cheese.

PA Warm-Up

Identifying Final Sounds

Say the words on the list below. Have students tell you the last sound of each word they hear. Example: tell (/l/)

wage (/j/)	much (/ch/)	which (/ch/)
got (/t/)	pet (/t/)	watch (/ch/)
Midge (/j/)	catch (/ch/)	nap (/p/)
cage (/j/)	miss (/s/)	page (/j/)

Word Work

You will need the following letter tiles for this Word Work activity: *ch, j, t, p, d, a, e, i*

Start word: at

Word list: chat, Chad, chap, chip, chep*, jep*, jet, jat*

Dictation

Write the following words in Elkonin boxes. Remember that digraphs stay together in one box.

1. jig
2. jab

3. chip
4. chat

Write the following words on the word lines. The ∿ will be located under the word line to remind students to include the digraph.

1. chap
2. jag

3. Chad

Write the following sentences on the sentence lines.

1. Look at the jet.

2. Jim and Chaz chat.

Consonants and Digraph *ch* & *j*: Decodable

Read and answer the questions.

Tricky Words: and, said, look, the, can, go

The Jet

Chip and Jed chat. Jed said, "Look at the jet, Chad."
Chad can look at the jet. Jed can look at the jet.
The big jet can go, go, go!

Comprehension

Students may need help with the italicized words.

What can the big jet do?

_____

- -

_____

Word Sort

Cut out the words and pictures. Then sort them under the appropriate header.

ch	***j***	chat	jab
		jig	
jet	chip		

Name: _____ Date: _____

Consonants and Digraph *ch* & *j*: Dictation

Elkonin Boxes

1.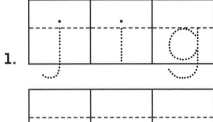

2.

3.

4.

Words   Score: /3 words

_____   _____   _____
- - - - - - - - - - - -   - - - - - - - - - - - -   - - - - - - - - - - - -

1. _____   2. _____   3. _____
   ~~~   ~~~

Sentences   Score: /8 words

_____
- -

1. _____

_____
- -

2. _____

Lesson 10 | Consonants *m & n*

Tips, Tricks, and Details

- The letters *m* and *n* are nasal letters. This means the sound for these letters comes from the nose. To demonstrate this, have students plug their noses while saying words that start with *m* or *n*.

- When *m* and *n* are positioned after a short *a*, their sounds change. Spelling and reading words with this pattern will be covered in Unit 2.

PA Warm-Up

Identifying Final Sounds

Say the words on the list below. Have students tell you the last sound of each word they hear. Example: pin /n/

ban (/n/)	Sam (/m/)	lamb (/m/)
Cam (/m/)	limb (/m/)	Jim (/m/)
kin (/n/)	dim (/m/)	fin (/n/)
men (/n/)	spin (/n/)	tin (/n/)

Word Work

You will need the following letter tiles for this Word Work activity: *n, e, t, m, a, g, p, i*

Start word: net

Word list: met, mat, mag, nag, nap, nip, pin, tin, ten, men

Vocabulary practice: nag, nip

Dictation

Write the following words in Elkonin boxes.

1. nap

2. nit

3. med

4. map

Write the following words on the word lines. The ~~ will be located under the word line to remind students to include the digraph.

1. chin

2. Meg

3. mat

Write the following sentences on the sentence lines.

1. I met Meg and Ned in the jet.

2. Can you get the net to Mag?

Consonants *m* & *n*: Decodable

Read the story. Draw a picture of one of the things Mav and Jen can do.

Tricky Words: and, by, the, a, can, all, day, to

Mav and Jen

Mav and Jen met by the mat. Mav and Jen sat to chat, chat, chat. Mav and Jen did chat all day.

Mav and Jen can get the mat. Mav and Jen can tap, tap, tap. Mav and Jen can tap all day.

Mav and Jen can get the mat and nap. Mav and Jen can nap all day.

Word Sort

Cut out the words and pictures. Then sort them under the appropriate header.

m	**n**	mag	nip	nag
nap	mid	met	men	net

Consonants *m* & *n*: Dictation

Elkonin Boxes

1. | n | a | p |

2. | | | |

3. | | | |

4. | | | |

Words

Score: /3 words

1. _____ ~~~

2. _____

3. _____

Sentences

Score: /15 words

1. _____

2. _____

Lesson 11 | Short o

PA Warm-Up

Identifying Final Sounds

Say the words on the list below. Have students tell you the last sound of each word they hear. Example: pod /d/

bot (/t/)	sop (/p/)	nose (/z/)
cod (/d/)	lot (/t/)	job (/b/)
con (/n/)	dose (/s/)	scoff (/f/)
mop (/p/)	spot (/t/)	log (/g/)

Word Work

You will need the following letter tiles for this Word Work activity: o, n, d, g, f, a, b, p, s

Start word: on

Word list: don, dog, fog, nog, nag, nab, nap, sap, sop, sod, sob

Vocabulary practice: don, sop, sod, sob

Dictation

Write the following words in Elkonin boxes.

1. bop   **3.** top

2. pod   **4.** got

Write the following words on the word lines.

1. fad   **3.** fob

2. dot

Write the following sentences on the sentence lines.

1. I did not sip the pop.   **2.** Tod can dot and jot.

Short *o*: Decodable

Decodable Comic Strip

Read and illustrate what's happening.

Tricky Words: my, a, and, the, can, be, all, day

My pop, Von, got a big dog and it is a big job.	The dog can be bad. It can beg and nip all day.	Von fed and did pet the dog. The dog did not beg and nip.

Word Sort

Cut out the words and pictures. Then sort them under the appropriate header.

Initial /ŏ/	Medial /ŏ/	on	dog	not
op	nod	pot	sob	fog

Name: _____ Date: _____

Short *o*: Dictation

Elkonin Boxes

1.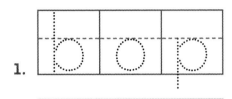

3.

2.

4.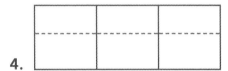

Words
Score: /3 words

1. _____   2. _____   3. _____

Sentences
Score: /11 words

1. _____

2. _____

Lesson 12 | Consonants and Digraph *w*, *h*, & *wh*

Tips, Tricks, and Details

- In some dialects, the *wh* digraph has a breathy *h*. For the majority of areas, the *wh* sounds like /w/. We recommend teaching this lesson with your area's dialect in mind.

- The *w* spelling is far more common than the *wh* spelling. Try teaching the common *wh* words (who, what, when, where, why, which) as the *wh* question words to form a distinction between the two spellings.

PA Warm-Up

Identifying Final Sounds

Say the words on the list below. Have students tell you the last sound of each word they hear. Example: well /l/

hot (/t/)	hail (/l/)	him (/m/)
which (/ch/)	hutch (/ch/)	hop (/p/)
when (/n/)	wick (/k/)	wed (/d/)
hill (/l/)	whip (/p/)	whisk (/k/)

Word Work

You will need the following letter tiles for this Word Work activity: *w, wh, h, e, n, t, i, p, m, o*

Start word: when

Word list: whet, wet, wit, hit, hip, him, whim, whip, hip, hop, hot

Vocabulary practice: whet, whim

Dictation

Write the following words in Elkonin boxes.

1. which   **3.** hen

2. hem   **4.** wet

Write the following words on the word lines. The ～ will be located under the word line to remind students to include the digraph.

1. hog   **3.** when

2. web

Write the following sentences on the sentence lines.

1. Which hog can go to the wet bog?   **2.** When is the jig at the hut?

Consonants and Digraph *w*, *h*, & *wh*: Decodable

Read and illustrate what Hap did in the box below.

Tricky Words: the, no, do, said, to, one, and

Hap and the Hot Pot

The pot is hot, hot, hot! "No, Hap! Do not tip the hot pot!" the mom said to the dog. Hap did wag. Hap did one big wag and did tip the pot! The mat is hot and wet! The mom has to mop.

Word Sort

Cut out the words and pictures. Then sort them under the appropriate header.

w/wh	*h*	whim	hen	wit
web	hag	hog	had	whip

Name: _____ Date: _____

Consonants and Digraph *w*, *h*, & *wh*: Dictation

Elkonin Boxes

1.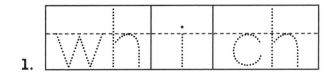

3. [empty Elkonin box with three cells]

2. [empty Elkonin box with three cells]

4. [empty Elkonin box with three cells]

Words   Score: /3 words

1. _____   2. _____   3. _____

Sentences   Score: /15 words

1. _____

2. _____

Lesson 13 | Consonants *l* & *r*

Tips, Tricks, and Details

- Both *l* and *r* can influence vowel sounds. This lesson will cover these sounds in the initial position.
- *R* can be an especially difficult sound for some students to pronounce correctly. Speech development charts suggest that clear *r* articulation should not be expected until six years of age.[6]

PA Warm-Up

Identifying Final Sounds

Say the words on the list below. Have students tell you the last sound of each word they hear. Example: pin /n/

well (/l/)	mull (/l/)	door (/r/)
sill (/l/)	will (/l/)	par (/r/)
for (/r/)	bar (/r/)	dill (/l/)
tar (/r/)	bill (/l/)	peer (/r/)

Word Work

You will need the following letter tiles for this Word Work activity: *l, r, d, i, a, p, o, b*

Start word: rad

Word list: lad, lap, rap, rip, lip, lop, lob, rob, rib

Vocabulary practice: rad, lop, lob

Dictation

Write the following words in Elkonin boxes.

1. rid   **3.** leg

2. rag   **4.** lot

Write the following words on the word lines. The ∿ will be located under the word line to remind students to include the digraph.

1. rich   **3.** lit

2. rot

Write the following sentences on the sentence lines.

1. The lab is rad.   **2.** Ren and Ron will rap on the log.

6 K. Crowe and S. McLeod, "Children's English Consonant Acquisition in the United States: A Review," *American Journal of Speech-Language Pathology* 29, no. 4 (2020), https://doi.org/10.1044/2020_AJSLP-19-00168.

Consonants *l* & *r*: Decodable

Read the story and underline the *l* and *r* words.

Tricky Words: a, the, by, will, see, but, said, like, she, to, of, and

Liz and the Cat

Liz sat on a log. The log is on the big lot by the den. A dog is in the den. Liz will see the dog. She will let the dog sit on the log. Liz will pet the dog, but the dog has a rat! "It is a rat!" said Liz. Liz did not like the rat. She will jog to the den. The rat bit the dog on the lip! The dog did not like the rat. The dog will jog to the den. The rat rid the log of Liz and the dog!

Word Sort

Cut out the words and pictures. Then sort them under the appropriate header.

l	*r*	lid	lab	rip
lip	rim	rich	rod	led

Consonants *l* & *r*: Dictation

Elkonin Boxes

1.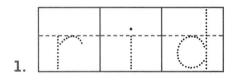

2.

3.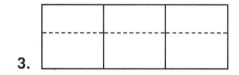

4.

Words   Score: /3 words

1. _____

2. _____

3. _____

Sentences   Score: /12 words

1. _____

_____

2. _____

_____

Lesson 14 | Short *u*

Tips, Tricks, and Details

- This is the last short vowel sound that students will learn. We suggest moving through this lesson slowly to ensure they have mastered all vowel sounds before moving on.

PA Warm-Up

Identifying Final Sounds

Say the words on the list below. Have students tell you the last sound of each word they hear. Example: pun /n/

bun (/n/)	sum (/m/)	hub (/b/)
cud (/d/)	rub (/b/)	mum (/m/)
mud (/d/)	puff (/f/)	fun (/n/)
muck (/k/)	spun (/n/)	ton (/n/)

Word Work

You will need the following letter tiles for this Word Work activity: *b, u, n, p, r, t, i, g, l, ch*

Start word: bun

Word list: pun, run, rut, but, bit, big, bug, rug, lug, chug, pug, pig, rig

Vocabulary practice: pun, rut, lug

Dictation

Write the following words in Elkonin boxes.

1. bud

2. jut

3. tub

4. much

Write the following words on the word lines.

1. bus

2. tug

3. dud

Write the following sentences on the sentence lines.

1. I got the sub and the chip bag.

2. Run to the mud hut!

Short *u*: Decodable

Read the story. Underline the short *u* words.

Tricky Words: a, and, he, like, to, the, down, be, will

Rod and Pup

Rod is a bug and he has a bud. It is Pup. Pup is not a bug, but he is a pug. Rod and Pup like to sit in the hot sun. Rod and Pup like to run. Rod and Pup will run up and down the rut. Pup will win, and Rod will get sad. Pup will hug Rod and get him gum! Rod will not be sad. It is fun in the sun!

Word Sort

Cut out the words and pictures. Then sort them under the appropriate header.

initial /ŭ/	medial /ŭ/	fun	pup	mum
rug	up	tug	nut	us
				✂ – – –

Name: _____ Date: _____

Short *u*: Dictation

Elkonin Boxes

1.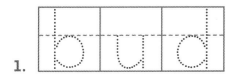

2.

3.

4.

Words   Score: /3 words

1. _____   2. _____   3. _____

Sentences   Score: /13 words

1. _____

_____

_____

2. _____

Spelling Rule | *c, k, & -ck*

Tips, Tricks, and Details

- Hard *c* & *k*: Hard *c* is used before consonants and the vowels *a*, *o*, and *u*. *K* is used before *e* and *i*.
- *-ck*: *-ck* is used at the end of a one-syllable word right after a short vowel. Use *k* in all other instances.

PA Warm-Up

Identifying Final Sounds

Say the words on the list below. Have students tell you the last sound of each word they hear. Example: sick /k/

duck (/k/)	kite (/t/)	yell (/l/)
steak (/k/)	lack (/k/)	hack (/k/)
race (/s/)	lake (/k/)	cell (/l/)
cap (/p/)	fur (/r/)	lace (/s/)

Word Work

You will need the following letter tiles for this Word Work activity: *l, u, ck, m, p, k, c, o, d, t, i*

Underlined words signify the need to change two tiles.

Start word: luck

Word list: muck, puck, pick, kick, kit, cut, cot, cod, kid, Kim

Vocabulary practice: muck

Dictation

Some of the following words may be included in the Word Sort. Students should cut out the Word Sort section before starting the dictation.

Write the following words in Elkonin boxes.

1. Jack

2. kin

3. cut

4. chick

Write the following words on the word lines. The ∿ will be located under the word line to remind students to include the digraph.

1. lack

2. cub

3. kick

Write the following sentence on the sentence line.

1. Cal and Kip kick the rock.

Name: _____ Date: _____

Spelling Rule *c*, *k*, & *-ck*: Dictation

Elkonin Boxes

1.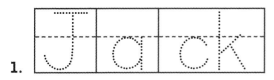

2. [empty Elkonin boxes]

3. [empty Elkonin boxes]

4. [empty Elkonin boxes]

Words   Score: /3 words

1. _____ ~~~

2. _____

3. _____ ~~~

Sentence   Score: /6 words

1. _____

Word Sort

Cut out the words and pictures. Then sort them under the appropriate header.

k	*c*	*-ck*	cab	cod
back	kin	pick	tuck	kid

Lesson 15 | Consonant *x*

Tips, Tricks, and Details

- The letter *x* is a borrower, which means it can make more than one sound. Most commonly, it sounds like a blend of /k/ and /s/, as in fix. In a few words, it can also sound like /z/, as in xylophone, or /gz/ as in exist.

- We do not recommend using Elkonin boxes for the *x* = /ks/ pattern because it may be confusing to some students. If you must use Elkonin boxes, have the students write the *x* across two boxes to show that it makes two sounds.

PA Warm-Up

Identifying Final Sounds

Say the words on the list below. Tell students the words will either end in an /s/ sound or a /ks/ sound, and that the /ks/ sound in these words is made by an *x*. Have the students tell you which endings hear with each word.

box (/ks/)	fix (/ks/)	fax (/ks/)
kiss (/s/)	max (/ks/)	rex (/ks/)
pass (/s/)	hiss (/s/)	guess (/s/)
pox (/ks/)	lass (/s/)	Tess (/s/)

Word Work

You will need the following letter tiles for this Word Work activity: *b, o, x, p, l, f, i, s, a, m*

Start word: box

Word list: pox, lox, ox, fox, fix, six, sax, fax, max, mix

Vocabulary practice: pox, lox

Dictation

Write the following words on the word lines.

1. ox   **4.** tux

2. tax   **5.** fix

3. hex   **6.** nix

Write the following sentences on the sentence lines.

1. Mix the wax in the cup.   **2.** The lox is in the box.

Consonant *x* Dictation

Words   Score: /6 Words

_____   _____   _____
- - - - - - - - - - - -   - - - - - - - - - - - -   - - - - - - - - - - - -
1. _____   3. _____   5. _____

_____   _____   _____
- - - - - - - - - - - -   - - - - - - - - - - - -   - - - - - - - - - - - -
2. _____   4. _____   6. _____

Sentences   Score: /12 words

_____
- -
1. _____

_____
- -
2. _____

Word Sort

Cut out the words and pictures. Then sort them under the appropriate header.

Ends with **X**	Ends with **s**	Ends with **ck**	ox	rock
mix	sis	fax	tick	pox

Lesson 16 | Consonant *y*

Tips, Tricks, and Details

- The letter *y* can be challenging for students because it can make both a consonant and a vowel sound. Typically, we hear the consonant *y* sound /y/, as in yellow, when it is at the beginning of a word. We hear a long /ī/ (fry) or /ē/ (happy) when it is at the end of a word or syllable. It can also make a short /ĭ/ sound (gym) when positioned in the middle of a word.

PA Warm-Up

Identifying Medial Sounds

Say the words on the list below. Have students tell you the medial (vowel) sound of each word they hear. Example: kit (/ĭ/)

bin (/ĭ/)	yip (/ĭ/)	yet (/ĕ/)
pat (/ă/)	mutt (/ŭ/)	nut (/ŭ/)
cot (/ŏ/)	vat (/ă/)	fin (/ĭ/)
yen (/ĕ/)	chip (/ĭ/)	pod (/ŏ/)

Word Work

You will need the following letter tiles for this Word Work activity: *y, e, s, t, n, ck, u, m, p, i*

Start word: yes

Word list: yet, yen, yeck*, yuck, yum, yup, yip, yep

Vocabulary Practice: yip, yen

Dictation

Write the following words in Elkonin boxes.

1. yuck   **2.** yip

Write the following words on the word lines.

1. yes   **3.** yum
2. yap

Write the following sentences on the sentence lines.

1. The dog will yip and yap.   **2.** Yes, I can hop!

Name: _____   Date: _____

Consonant *y*: Dictation

Elkonin Boxes

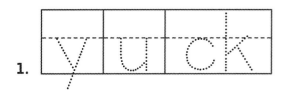

1.

2.

Words   Score: /3 words

_____   _____   _____

1. _____   2. _____   3. _____

Sentences   Score: /10 words

1. _____

_____

2. _____

Word Sort

Cut out the words and pictures. Then sort them under the appropriate header.

y	*r*	*l*	*c*	yes
cob	yak	lot	yet	rad

Lesson 17 | Digraph *qu*

Tips, Tricks, and Details

- *Q* is always paired with *u* in English words. While there are a few exceptions to this, all of these exceptions are words derived from other languages, namely Spanish, French, and Arabic. Because of this, we teach students to place the *q* and *u* together in one Elkonin box. Some teachers choose to draw a heart around them to show that they are always together.

- *Qu* can make two sounds. Its most common sound is /kw/, as in queen or question. It can also sound like /k/, as in clique or unique. This lesson will cover *qu* and its most common sound, /kw/.

PA Warm-Up

Identifying Medial Sounds

Say the words on the list below. Have students tell you the medial (vowel) sound of each word they hear. Example: bit (/ĭ/)

quit (/ĭ/)	chat (/ă/)	quell (/ĕ/)
queen (/ē/)	yen (/ĕ/)	queer (/ē/)
quest (/ĕ/)	fox (/ŏ/)	Quinn (/ĭ/)
quiz (/ĭ/)	pun (/ŭ/)	quad (/ŏ/)

Word Work

You will need the following letter tiles for this Word Work activity: *qu, i, z, p, t, ck, a, d*

Start word: quiz

Word list: quip, quit, quid, quick, quack

Vocabulary practice: quip, quid

Dictation

Some of the following words may be included in the Word Sort. Students should cut out the Word Sort section before starting the dictation.

Write the following words in Elkonin boxes.

1. Quin   **3.** quick

2. quack   **4.** quig*

Write the following words on the word lines. The ～ will be located under the word line to remind students to include the digraph.

1. quiz   **3.** quob*

2. quid

Write the following sentence on the sentence line.

1. Quin and I had a pop quiz.

Name: _____   Date: _____

Digraph *qu*: Dictation

Elkonin Boxes

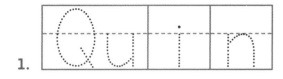

1.

2.

3.

4.

Words   Score: /3 words

1. _____   2. _____   3. _____

Sentence   Score: /7 words

1. _____

Word Sort

Cut out the words and pictures. Then sort them under the appropriate header.

qu	*k*	*w*	quiz	win
quit	kick	quack	kit	wed

Lesson 18 | Soft *th* & Hard *th*

Tips, Tricks, and Details

• The *th* digraph can be soft, as in think, and hard, as in **these**. The soft *th* pattern is more common.

PA Warm-Up

Identifying Targeted Sounds

Say the words below. Have your students tell you if the /th/ sound is voiced (like *then*), or unvoiced (like *thick*). Ask them to put their hands on their throats to feel for the sound.

thin (unvoiced)	this (voiced)	with (unvoiced)
thumb (unvoiced)	them (voiced)	moth (unvoiced)
then (voiced)	than (voiced)	bath (unvoiced)
these (voiced)	path (unvoiced)	death (unvoiced)

Word Work

You will need the following letter tiles for this Word Work activity: *th, i, ck, n, a, e, m, p, b*

Start word: thick

Word list: thin, then, them, the, eth*, ath*, math, path, bath

Vocabulary practice: path

Dictation

Write the following words in Elkonin boxes.

1. with

2. then

3. guth*

4. thib*

Write the following words on the word lines. The ⌇ will be located under the word line to remind students to include the digraph.

1. hath

2. moth

3. thin

Write the following sentences on the sentence lines.

1. The moth is in the bath.

2. This is the path to the math quiz.

Name: _____ Date: _____

Soft *th* & Hard *th*: Decodable

Read and underline the *th* words. Draw a picture of a scene from the story.

Tricky Words: a, day, first, will, the, have, be

Lex and Seth Have a Fun Day

Seth has a pet cat, Lex. Lex has a big day. First, Lex will sit in the wet mud. Then, Lex will sit in the hot sun on the deck. Then, Lex will run on the rock path with Seth. Then, Lex will have a bath. Then, Seth and Lex will have a nap. It will be a fun day!

Word Sort

Cut out the words and pictures. Then sort them under the appropriate header.

Soft /th/	Hard /th/	this	thin	math
then	bath	them	thick	the

UNIT 1: CONSONANTS, CONSONANT DIGRAPHS, AND SHORT VOWELS   65

Soft *th* & Hard *th*: Dictation

Elkonin Boxes

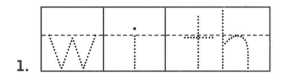

1.

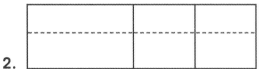

2.

3.

4.

Words   Score: /3 words

1. _____ 2. _____ 3. _____

Sentences   Score: /14 words

1.

2.

Lesson 19 | Consonant Digraphs *sh* & *zsh*

Tips, Tricks, and Details

- The unvoiced /sh/ sound can be represented by *sh* (shell), *ch* (chef), and *ti/ci* (vacation, delicious).
- The voiced /zsh/ sound can be represented by *sh* (cashmere), *sure* (treasure), *si* (television), and *g/j* (rouge, dijon).
- This lesson will cover reading and spelling words with the most common sound and spelling, *sh* spells /sh/. It will include phonemic awareness activities for both sounds.

PA Warm-Up

Identifying Targeted Sounds

Say each word on the list below. Have students tell you if they hear a /sh/ (like ship), or a /zsh/ (like beige).

bash (/sh/)	leisure (/zsh/)	lash (/sh/)
vision (/zsh/)	wish (/sh/)	shack (/sh/)
shin (/sh/)	Asia (/zsh/)	pleasure (/zsh/)
shall (/sh/)	collage (/zsh/)	short (/sh/)

Word Work

You will need the following letter tiles for this Word Work activity: *sh, o, t, p, i, n, ch, th, ck, a*

Start word: shot

Word list: shop, ship, shin, chin, thin, thick, chick, chock, shock, shack

Vocabulary practice: chock, shock, shack

Dictation

Write the following words in Elkonin boxes.

1. mesh

2. shun

3. rash

4. shed

Write the following words on the word lines. The ∿ will be located under the word line to remind students to include the digraph.

1. lush

2. shuck

3. mash

Write the following sentences on the sentence lines.

1. You can get the fish at the shop.

2. She can go to the big bash.

Name: _____   Date: _____

Consonant Digraphs *sh* & *zsh*: Decodable

Read and underline the *sh* words. Draw a picture of a scene from the story.

Tricky Words: I, to, go, a, said, the, and, look, will, see, can, come, be

A Big Ship Wish

"I wish to go on a big ship!" said Cash. Cash will pack a fun top. Then, he will go to the shop to get a sun hat. He will sit on the deck and look at the fish. Cash will see if his bud, Josh, can come with him! It will be fun on the big ship!

Word Sort

Cut out the words and pictures. Then sort them under the appropriate header.

sh	*ch*	*th*	shun	thus
chap	shut	cash	thud	chit

Name: _____   Date: _____

Consonant Digraphs *sh* & *zsh*: Dictation

Elkonin Boxes

1.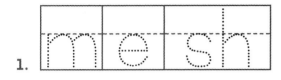

2.

3.

4.

Words   Score: /3 words

1. _____ 2. _____ 3. _____

Sentences   Score: /15 words

1. _____

_____

_____

2. _____

_____

_____

Spelling Rule | The Doubling Rule *ff, ss, ll,* & zz

Tips, Tricks, and Details

- If a one-syllable word with a short vowel sound ends with *s, l, f,* or *z*, double it! *Exceptions*:
  - shortened words (bus, short for omnibus; gas, short for gasoline)
  - words with long vowels (gross, troll)
  - glued sounds (ball)
  - endings with /z/ sound (his, was, is, has)
  - yes, this, plus

PA Warm-Up

Identifying Medial Sounds

Say the words on the list below. Have students tell you the medial (vowel) sound of each word. Example: puff (/ŭ/)

pass (/ă/)	lass (/ă/)	buzz (/ŭ/)
yell (/ĕ/)	mull (/ŭ/)	fell (/ĕ/)
kiss (/ĭ/)	mess (/ĕ/)	fill (/ĭ/)
toss (/ŏ/)	doll (/ŏ/)	muff (/ŭ/)

Word Work

You will need the following letter tiles for this Word Work activity: *c, u, m, b, f, e, d, i, p, ss, ff, ll, zz*

Start word: cuff

Word list: muff, buff, buzz, fuzz, fuss, fess, fell, dell, dill, pill

Vocabulary practice: cuff, buff, fess, dill

Dictation

Write the following words in Elkonin boxes.

1. tell

2. fizz

3. loss

4. miff

Write the following words on the word lines.

1. will

2. less

3. puff

Write the following sentence on the sentence line.

1. Can you get the fuzz off of the doll?

Name: _____   Date: _____

The Doubling Rule *ff*, *ss*, *ll*, & *zz*: Dictation

Elkonin Boxes

1.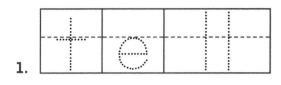

2. (empty boxes)

3. (empty boxes)

4. (empty boxes)

Words   Score: /3 words

1. _____   2. _____   3. _____

Sentence   Score: /9 words

1. _____

Word Sort

Cut out the words and pictures. Then sort them under the appropriate header.

ff	*ll*	*ss*	*zz*	fizz
moss	jazz	pass	chill	puff
				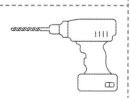

Spelling Rule | Plural Spelling Rule -s, -es, & -lves

Tips, Tricks, and Details

- If a word ends in /sh/, /ch/, /s/, /zsh/, /j/, /x/, or /z/, add -es to form the plural.
- Sometimes, if a word ends in f, you must change it to v and add -es.
- For all other words, just add -s. Remember that s can sound like /s/ or /z/.

  Exceptions: This rule does not apply to nouns that have no change (deer-deer), or irregular nouns (tooth-teeth).
- Plurals ending in y (puppy-puppies) are covered later in our book, *Teach Reading with Orton-Gillingham*.

PA Warm-Up

Identifying Parts of Words

Say the plural word on the list below. Have students tell you the base word of each word. Example: puffs (**puff**)

watches (watch)	fills (fill)	wages (wage)
halves (half)	limbs (limb)	glasses (glass)
kilts (kilt)	dims (dim)	quizzes (quiz)
dogs (dog)	wishes (wish)	babies (baby)

Word Work

You will need the following letter tiles for this Word Work activity: s, e, b, o, x, f, c, a, sh, l, d

This sort will require students to change more than one letter tile for -es endings.

Start word: box

Word list: boxes, foxes, fox, fob, fobs, cobs, cabs, cab, cash, <u>cashes</u>, <u>lashes</u>, lash, lad, lads

Vocabulary practice: fob, cob, lad

Dictation

> Write the following words on the word lines. The ⌇ will be located under the word line to remind students to include the digraph.

1. cups

2. chicks

3. wishes

> Write the following sentences on the sentence lines.

1. Can you pick up the messes in the shacks?

2. The kids run to the beds.

The Doubling Rule -s, -es, & -lves: Dictation

Words   Score: /3 words

_____   _____   _____

- - - - - - - - - - - - - -   - - - - - - - - - - - - - -   - - - - - - - - - - - - - -

1. _____   2. _____   3. _____

Sentences   Score: /15 words

_____

- -

1. _____

_____

- -

2. _____

Word Sort

Cut out the words and pictures. Then sort them under the appropriate header.

Add -s	Add -es	moss	rush	tab
mash	tick	sip	thin	tax
chop	fax	toss	pass	puff

Unit 2: Blends and Glued Sounds

Using Elkonin Boxes with Consonant Blends, Welded Sounds, and Digraphs

Elkonin boxes are separated by sound; therefore, each sound in a word gets its own box.

This means that the consonants in blends are separated because it is possible to hear each sound clearly in a consonant blend. Digraphs (*sh, th, ch, -ck, wh, -tch*), doubled letters (*-ff, -ss, -ll,* and *-zz*) are kept together in one box. We also recommend teaching students to keep glued sounds (*an, am, al, all, -ng,* and *-nk*) together in one box since the consonant influences and changes the vowel sound, making it very different from its typical sound.

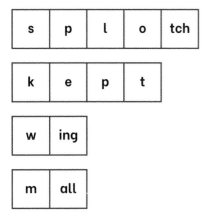

Spelling Rules Covered in This Unit

-ct Rule: If there is a /kt/ sound at the end of a word, it is spelled with a *-ct*. Words are never spelled with a *-kt* ending.

-ch/-tch: When a word ends in the /ch/ sound, use *-tch* if it follows a short vowel. Use *-ch* if it comes after a long vowel or consonant.

Exceptions: much, such, rich, and attach

Which sight words that are not yet decodable should my students know before starting this unit?

and	no	them
the	all	first
be	of	come
look	is	have
said	day	make
you	my	down
can	to	how
go	she	or
I	he	may
so	was	than
do	one	out
we	two	more
by	like	
a	see	

Which new and not-yet-decodable sight words will my students see during this unit?

what	an	use
from	for	there
who	your	been
her	are	many

What other information should I know?

We recommend having your student(s) read the decodable passage before the dictation practice. Also, in some lessons, the Word Sort activity is below the dictation page. We suggest cutting off that section before completing the dictation practice, as some of the words are duplicated.

Lesson 1 | Initial 2-Letter Blends

Tips, Tricks, and Details

- Review digraphs before completing this lesson. Explain that digraphs make one (often new) sound, while blends are two adjacent letters and have two distinct sounds

PA Warm-Up

Phoneme Blending

Verbally separate all of the sounds in the following words. Then have students tell you the whole word. Example: /n/ /u/ /t/ (nut)

/sh/ / ĭ / /p/ (ship)	/f/ / ŭ / /n/ (fun)	/t/ /r/ / ŭ / /k/ (truck)
/s/ / ă / /t/ (sat)	/c/ /l/ / ă / /p/ (clap)	/f/ /l/ / ă / /p/ (flap)
/th/ / ĭ / /k/ (thick)	/t/ /w/ / ĭ / /l/ (twill)	/s/ /l/ / ō / (slow)
/wh/ / ĕ / /n/ (when)	/sh/ /r/ / ŭ / /g/ (shrug)	/s/ /l/ / ŭ / /m/ (slum)

Word Work

Instruct the students to begin with the start word. Then go through the list in order by instructing students to build each word with their letter tiles. Students will change one or two tiles at a time. Refer to page 150 for our letter tiles or for tiles in color, visit our website (www.treetopseducation.com/teach-reading). Nonsense words will be marked with a star, and words that require two tile changes will be underlined.

You will need the following letter tiles for this Word Work activity: c, a, p, l, f, s, o, t, sh, r, d, i

Start word: cap

Word list: clap, flap, slap, slop, stop, top, shop, cop, crop, drop, drip, dip

Dictation

Write the following words in Elkonin boxes.

1. dress   **3.** grab

2. flip   **4.** sniff

Write the following words on the word lines.

1. glum   **3.** frill

2. class

Write the following sentences on the sentence lines.

1. The grim crab was in the grass.   **2.** Brad will snap with his pal.

Initial 2-Letter Blends: Decodable

Tricky Words: like, to, and, all, day, be, he

Brad and Stan

Brad is a twin. Stef is his twin. Brad likes to fish. Stef likes to snack. Brad will grab his rod and Stef will grab his snack bag. Brad will fish all day. He will spot a crab and a frog. Stef will snack on a plum and fig. It will be a fun day!

Comprehension

What does Brad like to do? What does Stef like to do? Draw a picture in the box below.

Initial 2-Letter Blends: Dictation

Elkonin Boxes

1. | | | | |

3. | | | | |

2. | | | | |

4. | | | | |

Words   Score: /3 words

_____   _____   _____

- - - - - - - - - - - -   - - - - - - - - - - - -   - - - - - - - - - - - -

1. _____   2. _____   3. _____

Sentences   Score: /13 words

_____

- -

1. _____

_____

- -

2. _____

Word Sort

Cut out the words. Then sort them under the appropriate header.

Initial Blend	Initial Digraph	chick	blab	slob
thin	clad	brag	glad	sped
when	fled	chin	scat	chuck

Lesson 2 | Initial 3-Letter Blends

Tips, Tricks, and Details

- This lesson includes three-letter blends (*scr-*, *spl-*, *str-*, and *squ-*) and consonant trigraphs, three-letter blends that contain a digraph (*shr-*, *thr-*, and *-nth*).

- *Sch-* is also a consonant trigraph (school, schedule, scheme, etc.), but the hard *ch* /k/ sound is not covered until Unit 9 in *Teach Reading with Orton-Gillingham*.

- Words with the *-nth* trigraph pattern will not be included until students have learned final consonant blends.

PA Warm-Up

Phoneme Blending

Verbally separate all of the sounds in the words below. Then have your students tell you the whole word. Example: /s/ /k/ /i/ /p/ (skip)

/c/ /r/ / ă / /sh/ (crash)	/ch/ / ă / /t/ (chat)	/s/ /k/ / ĭ / /n/ (skin)
/f/ /l/ / ĭ / /p/ (flip)	/t/ /r/ / ĭ / /k/ (trick)	/t/ /r/ / ŭ / /k/ (truck)
/sh/ / ă / /k/ (shack)	/g/ /r/ / ă / /b/ (grab)	/s/ /p/ /l/ / ă / /t/ (splat)
/g/ /l/ / ă / /s/ (glass)	/f/ /l/ / ă / /p/ (flap)	/sh/ /r/ / ŭ / /g/ (shrug)
/b/ /r/ / ĭ / /m/ (brim)	/t/ /r/ / ĭ / /m/ (trim)	/s/ /qu/ / ĭ / /d/ (squid)
/s/ /l/ / ă / /sh/ (slash)	/th/ /r/ / ō / (throw)	/s/ /t/ /r/ / ĭ / /c/ t/ (strict)

Word Work

You will need the following letter tiles for this Word Work activity: *s, i, t, p, l, a, sh, r, c, th*

Start word: sit

Word list: spit, split, splat, spat, sat, sash, slash, lash, rash, crash, trash, thrash

Dictation

> Write the following words in Elkonin boxes. Remember that digraphs stay together in one box.

1. split

2. throb

3. shrug

4. squish

> Write the following words on the word lines. The ∿— symbol will be included to indicate a trigraph, a three-letter blend that contains a digraph.

1. shrill

2. splash

3. sprig

> Write the following sentences on the sentence lines.

1. That dog will thrash in the bath.

2. Split the shrimp snack with Fred.

Initial 3-Letter Blends: Decodable

Decodable Comic Strip

Read and illustrate what is happening in the story.

Tricky Words: of, the, from, no, more

Greg has a black truck. It has lots of mud spots.	Greg will grab the wet rag from the bin. *Squish!*

Greg will scrub the black truck. *Splish!*	Greg will drop the rag in the bin. *Splash!* No more mud spots!

Initial 3-Letter Blends: Dictation

Elkonin Boxes

1. | | | | | |
|---|---|---|---|---|
| | | | | |

3. | | | | |
|---|---|---|---|
| | | | |

2. | | | | |
|---|---|---|---|
| | | | |

4. | | | | |
|---|---|---|---|
| | | | |

Words   Score: /3 words

1. _____   2. _____   3. _____

Sentences   Score: /13 words

1. _____

2. _____

Word Sort

Cut out the words. Then sort them under the appropriate header.

Blends	**Trigraphs**	shrill	thrill	squish
splat	split	squid	throb	struck
sprig	shrub	thrush	strum	

Lesson 3 | Final Blends

Tips, Tricks, and Details

- In this lesson, students will see words with consonant blends in the beginning and final position of words.

- The blends -nk, -rd, and -rk are not included in this lesson because the vowel is influenced by the n and r. These patterns are included in later lessons.

PA Warm-Up

Phoneme Segmentation

Say the words below. Have students tell you the sounds in the word. Example: make (/m/ /ā/ /k/)

catch /c/ / ă / /ch/	bat /b/ / ă / /t/	spin /s/ /p/ / ĭ / /n/
shack /sh/ / ă / /k/	clot /c/ /l/ / ŏ / /t/	trip /t/ /r/ / ĭ / /p/
sock /s/ / ŏ / /k/	them /th/ / ĕ / /m/	fast /f/ / ă / /s/ /t/
thin /th/ / ĭ / /n/	crack /c/ /r/ / ă / /k/	shift /sh/ / ĭ / /f/ /t/

Word Work

You will need the following letter tiles for this Word Work activity: g, a, p, s, r, f, c, t, i, l, w, e

Start word: gap

Word list: gasp, rasp, raft, craft, graft, grift, rift, sift, silt, wilt, welt

Dictation

Write the following words in Elkonin boxes. Remember that digraphs stay together in one box.

1. weld
2. past

3. send
4. crimp

Write the following words on the word lines.

1. runt
2. clump

3. silk

Write the following sentences on the sentence lines.

1. The men had on black felt kilts.

2. The doc had to crack the cast.

Final Blends: Decodable

Tricky Words: an, he, the, and, all, can, do, to, by, out, of

Dash and Frost

Dash is an elf. He is in bed, sick with a bug. He has slept and slept. He has not left his tent. All Dash can do is sip milk, but it will not help.

His elf bud, Frost, stops by his tent. Frost has a gift. It is the best snack. It is a kelp broth. Dash sips the broth.

"Yum!" grins Dash. In just ten sips, Dash is out of the bed! Dash hugs Frost. Dash is on the mend!

Comprehension

Students may need help with the italicized words.

1. *Why* is Dash in bed?

_____

- -

_____

2. *How* did Frost help Dash?

_____

- -

_____

Final Blends: Dictation

Elkonin Boxes

1. | | | | |

2. | | | | |

3. | | | |

4. | | | | |

Words

Score: ___ /3 words

1. _____   2. _____   3. _____

Sentences

Score: ___ /14 words

1. _____

2. _____

Word Sort

Cut out the words. Then sort them under the appropriate header.

Initial Blend	Final Blend	**Both**	plus	splint
dress	pulp	stilt	crest	mast
rift	slept	grim	primp	

Spelling Rule | -*ct* Ending

Tips, Tricks, and Details

- -*ct* Rule: If there is a /kt/ sound at the end of a word, it is spelled with a -*ct*. Words are never spelled with a -*kt* ending.

- This pattern is seen more at the end of multisyllabic words ending with -*ct* (react, erupt, collect, etc.). There are very few one-syllable words with this pattern.

PA Warm-Up

Phoneme Segmentation

Say the words on the list below. Have students tell you the sounds in the words. Notice that there are several words ending with a -*cked* spelling. You may want to mention this to students who have been introduced to the -*ed* suffix. Example: fact (/f/ /a/ /k/ /t/)

lacked /l/ / ă / /k/ /t/	bloat /b/ /l/ / ō / /t/	spice /s/ /p/ / ī / /s/
sack /s/ / ă / /k/	slot /s/ /l/ / ŏ / /t/	flip /f/ /l/ / ĭ / /p/
sob /s/ / ŏ / /b/	theme /th/ / ē / /m/	cast /c/ / ă / /s/ /t/
grin /g/ /r/ / ĭ / /n/	cracked /c/ /r/ / ă / /k/ /t/	strict /s/ /t/ /r/ / ĭ / /k/ /t/

Word Work

You will need the following letter tiles for this Word Work activity: *p, a, t, c, f, t, r, e, s*

Start word: pat

Word list: pact, fact, tact, tract, ract*, act, ect*, sect

Vocabulary practice: pact, tact, sect

Dictation

Write the following words in Elkonin boxes.

1. act

2. strict

Write the following word on the word lines.

1. duct

Write the following sentences on the sentence lines.

1. Can you tell me a fun fact?

2. The duct has dust in it.

-ct Ending: Dictation

Elkonin Boxes

1. | | | |
|---|---|---|

2. | | | | | | |
|---|---|---|---|---|---|

Words

Score: /1 word

1. _____

Sentences

Score: /13 words

1. _____

2. _____

Spelling Rule -*ch*/-*tch*

Tips, Tricks, and Details

- -*ch*/-*tch* Rule: When a word ends in the /ch/ sound, use -*tch* if it follows a short vowel. Use -*ch* if it comes after a long vowel or consonant.

  Exceptions: much, such, rich, and attach.

PA Warm-Up

Phoneme Segmentation

Say the words below. Have students tell you the sounds in the words.

cinch (/s/ / ĭ / /n/ /ch/)	leech /l/ / ē / /ch/	coach /c/ / ō / /ch/
fact /f/ / ă / /c/ /t/	thatch /th/ / ă / /ch/	witch /w/ / ĭ / /ch/
duct /d/ / ŭ / /c/ /t/	batch /b/ / ă / /t/ /ch/	munch /m/ / ŭ / /n/ /ch/
much /m/ / ŭ / /ch/	gulch /g/ /ŭ/ /l/ /ch/	
pitch /p/ / ĭ / /ch/	teach /t/ / ē / /ch/	

Word Work

You will need the following letter tiles for this Word Work activity: *ch, tch, g, u, l, m, n, b, e, s, k, f, i, w, t*

Start word: gulch

Word list: mulch, munch, bunch, bench, <u>stench</u>, <u>sketch</u>, fetch, etch, itch, witch

Vocabulary practice: gulch, stench, etch

Dictation

Write the following words in Elkonin boxes. Remember that *ch* and *tch* should stay together in one box since they make one sound.

1. lunch   **3.** belch

2. hatch   **4.** hitch

Write the following words on the word lines. The —∿ symbol will be included to indicate a trigraph, a three-letter blend that contains a digraph.

1. hunch   **3.** latch

2. stitch

Write the following sentences on the sentence lines.

1. The finch will sit on the branch.   **2.** Dig the ditch for the crops.

-ch/ -tch: Dictation

Elkonin Boxes

1. ☐☐☐☐

2. ☐☐☐

3. ☐☐☐☐

4. ☐☐☐

Words   Score: /3 words

1. _____ ⎯〰

2. _____ ⎯〰

3. _____ ⎯〰

Sentences   Score: /13 words

1. _____

2. _____

Word Sort

Cut out the words. Then sort them under the appropriate header.

-ch	*-tch*	patch	bunch	retch
crunch	Dutch	ranch	mulch	zilch
punch	catch	winch	match	hitch

Lesson 4 | Glued Sounds -*am* & -*an*

Tips, Tricks, and Details

- We recommend teaching *am* and *an* as "glued sounds." When an *a* is followed by an *m* or *n*, it becomes a nasal sound.

- To reinforce this, instruct students to plug their noses while saying regular short *a* words like *cat*, *bad*, and *lab*. Then instruct them to say nasal *a* words like *can*, *plan*, and *sham*. They should feel the nasal *a* coming from their noses while saying those words.

PA Warm-Up

Phoneme Segmentation

Say the words below. Have students tell you the sounds in the word. Example: ram /r/ /am/

yam /y/ /am/	sham /sh/ /am/	bank /b/ /an/ /k/
slam /s/ /l/ /am/	Dan /d/ /an/	span /s/ /p/ /an/
pan /p/ /an/	Sam /s/ /am/	clam /c/ /l/ /am/
cram /k/ /r/ /am/	plant /p/ /l/ /an/ /t/	clamp /c/ /l/ /am/ /p/

*We suggest keeping *am* and *an* together during segmentation because the *a* is nasal when followed by an *m* or *n*.

Word Work

You will need the following letter tiles for this Word Work activity: *c, am, p, l, an, s, f, t*

Start word: camp

Word list: clamp, lamp, amp, am, an, pan, span, scan, can, fan, tan

Vocabulary practice: clamp, amp, span

Dictation

Write the following words in Elkonin boxes. Remember that *am* and *an* should stay together in one box since they make a distinct sound when paired.

1. Jan

2. swam

3. hand

4. sham

Write the following words on the word lines. The ‾GS‾ symbol will be located under the word line to remind students to include the glued sound.

1. van

2. plan

3. ram

Write the following sentences on the sentence lines.

1. Can you cram for the test?

2. The man will get the yam and ham at the shop.

Glued Sounds *-am* & *-an*: Decodable

Decodable Comic Strip

Read and illustrate what's happening in the comic.

Tricky Words: have, to, make, for, he, the, you

Chef Cam has a test. He will have to make a lunch for his boss, Pam.	Cam has a plan. Cam will cram for the test.

He will put yams and a ham in the pan. Then, Cam will add a plum jam.	Pam bit the yam and ham with the plum jam. Pam tells Cam, "Yum! You pass the test!"

Glued Sounds *-am*, *-an*: Dictation

Elkonin Boxes

1. [|]

2. [| |]

3. [| |]

4. [|]

Words   Score: /3 words

1. _____   2. _____   3. _____

GS   GS   GS

Sentences   Score: /17 words

1. _____

_____

2. _____

Word Sort

Cut out the words. Then sort them under the appropriate header.

-am	*-an*	cram	than	clan
pram	plan	dam	scam	ban
ran	pam	gram	slam	

Lesson 5 | Glued Sounds -*al* & -*all*

Tips, Tricks, and Details

- The letter *l* can influence vowel sounds, especially when it is preceded by *a*. Because of this, we recommend teaching *al* and *all* as glued units rather than as individual phonemes.

- The *a* in *all* and *almost* often sounds like a short /o/. Some students may notice that in some *al* patterns, the sound is more like a short /u/. This can be explained by schwa (the vowel sound in an unaccented syllable).

- The suffix -*al* means "relating to" (historical, theatrical, etc.).

PA Warm-Up

Phoneme Segmentation

Say the words below. Have students tell you the sounds in the words. Example: ball /b/ /all/

fall /f/ /all/	tall /t/ /all/	scald /s/ /c/ /al/ /d/
mall /m/ /all/	pan /p/ /an/	walls /w/ /all/ /z/
ham /h/ /am/	halt /h/ /al/ /t/	salt /s/ /al/ /t/
stall /s/ /t/ /all/	small /s/ /m/ /all/	calls /c/ /all/ /z/

*We suggest keeping *al* and *all* together during segmentation. If you choose to keep these letters separate, be sure to remind your students that *a* does not make its typical short /a/ sound when followed by an *l*.

Word Work

You will need the following letter tiles for this Word Work activity: *c, b, all, s, t, h, m, t, f, w*

Start word: call

Word list: ball, hall, mall, small, stall, tall, fall, falls, walls

Vocabulary practice: halt, stall

Dictation

> Write the following words in Elkonin boxes. Remember that *all* and *al* should stay together in one box since they make a distinct sound when paired.

1. ball

2. wall

3. scald

4. squall* (*A reminder that we place *q* and *u* together in one box.)

> Write the following words on the word lines. The $\overline{\text{GS}}$ symbol will be located under the word line to remind students to include the glued sound.

1. gall

2. fall

3. malt

> Write the following sentences on the sentence lines.

1. Will you sip that malt?

2. The kid will toss the ball on the wall.

Name: _____   Date: _____

Glued Sounds *-al* & *-all* Decodable

Tricky Words: to, the, was, he, of, no, have, go, I, see, do, you, like, said, she, are

A Trip to the Mall

When Grant was six, he was small. He had lots of pants that fit him. Grant is ten and he is tall. He has no pants that fit! Grant and his mom have to go to the mall.

"I see black pants. Do you like them?" his mom asks.

"I can see if I do," Grant said. Grant grabs the pants and struts to a stall to see if the pants fit.

"Help!" he calls.

His mom runs to the stall. She has a big grin. "Did you fall?" she asks.

"Yes," Grant said as he sat on the rug with the pants stuck on his legs. "The pants are a bit small."

Comprehension

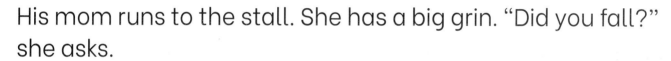

Students may need help with the italicized word.

1. *How* did Grant's pants fit him?

_____

- -

_____

Glued Sounds *-al* & *-all*: Dictation

Elkonin Boxes

1. | | |
|---|---|

2. | | |
|---|---|

3. | | | |
|---|---|---|

4. | | |
|---|---|

Words   Score: /3 words

1. _____   2. _____   3. _____

GS   GS   GS

Sentences   Score: /14 words

1. _____

_____

2. _____

Word Sort

Cut out the words. Then sort them under the appropriate header.

-al	*-all*	gall	small	all	alt
salt	stall	malt	hall	halt	tall
stall	waltz	squall	fall		

Lesson 6 | Glued Sound -*ng*

Tips, Tricks, and Details

- We teach /ing/, /ang/, /ung/, and /ong/ as glued sounds (along with /am/, /an/, /all/, /al/, /ink/, /ank/, /unk/, and /onk/). This means that we encourage students to keep these patterns as glued units rather than individual phonemes.

PA Warm-Up

Phoneme Segmentation

Say the words below. Have students tell you the sounds in the words. Example: sang /s/ /ang/

fang /f/ /ang/	sung /s/ /ung/	long /l/ /ong/
ping /p/ /ing/	pang /p/ /ang/	stung /s/ /t/ /ung/
sting /s/ /t/ /ing/	ding /d/ /ing/	long /l/ /ong/
lung /l/ /ung/	dung /d/ /ung/	bang /b/ /ang/

*We suggest keeping /ing/, /ang/, /ung/, and /ong/ together during segmentation as glued sounds. If you choose to keep the vowel separate from the -*ng*, be sure to remind your students that the vowel sounds may sound slightly different when paired with the -*ng*.

Word Work

You will need the following letter tiles for this Word Work activity: *ang, ung, ing, ong, th, s, r, l, t, b*

Start word: thing

Word list: sing, ring, rung, sung, song, long, tong, tang, rang, bang

Vocabulary practice: rung (ladder), tong, tang

Dictation

Write the following words in Elkonin boxes. Remember that glued sounds should stay together in one box since they make a distinct sound when paired.

1. bring

2. stung

3. bang

4. strong

Write the following words on the word lines. The ‾‾GS‾‾ and ⌣ symbols will be located under the word line to remind students to include the glued sound and digraph, respectively.

1. prong

2. swung

3. thing

Write the following sentences on the sentence lines.

1. Cal will sing the song.

2. Can you bring me the tongs?

Glued Sound *-ng*: Decodable

Tricky Words: like, to, the, of, first, day, he, there, was, down, see, what, said, my, for, how

King Ming and the Dog

King Ming likes to run the path to the top of the hill. On the first day of spring, as he treks to the path, there is a bang, bang, bang! King Ming runs down the hill to see what it was. He sees a hut, a dog, and a gong.

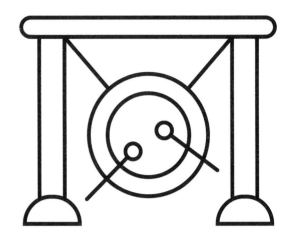

"What is with the gong?" King Ming asks the dog.

"I hung it next to my hut to help my bud, Ox. He went for a trek and got lost," said the dog.

"How sad! How can I help?" King Ming asks the dog.

"Are you strong? Can you help me bring the gong to the top of the hill? Then, Ox can see me and the gong!"

King Ming and the dog bring the gong up the hill. The dog rings the gong. Bang! Bang! Just then, the dog sees Ox and runs to hug him! King Ming is glad.

Comprehension

Students may need help with the italicized word.

1. *How* did King Ming help the dog?

_____

- -

_____

Glued Sound -ng: Dictation

Elkonin Boxes

1. | | | |

3. | | |

2. | | | |

4. | | | | |

Words   Score: /3 words

1. _____
   GS

2. _____
   GS

3. ~~~_____
   GS

Sentences   Score: /11 words

1. _____

_____

2. _____

Word Sort

Cut out the words. Then sort them under the appropriate header.

-ing	*-ang*	*-ong*	*-ung*	wing	clung
king	pong	sung	hang	lung	swing
dung	fang	tong	slung	clang	ding

Lesson 7 | Glued Sound -*nk*

Tips, Tricks, and Details

- We teach /ink/, /ank/, /unk/, and /onk/ as glued sounds (along with /am/, /an/, /all/, /al/, /ing/, /ang/, /ung/, and /ong/). This means that we encourage students to keep these patterns as glued units rather than individual phonemes.

PA Warm-Up

Phoneme Segmentation

Say the words below. Have students tell you the sounds in the words. Example: sank /s/ /ank/

thank /th/ /ank/	trunk /t/ /r/ /unk/	honk /h/ /onk/
mink /m/ /ink/	Hank /h/ /ank/	thunk /th/ /unk/
stink /s/ /t/ /ink/	link /l/ /ink/	bonk /b/ /onk/
junk /j/ /unk/	funk /f/ /unk/	bank /b/ /ank/

*We suggest keeping /ink/, /ank/, /unk/, and /onk/ together during segmentation as glued sounds. If you choose to keep the vowel separate from the *nk*, be sure to remind your students that the vowel sounds may sound slightly different when paired with the *nk*.

Word Work

You will need the following letter tiles for this Word Work activity: *ank, unk, ink, onk, th, t, r, p, f, d, b, h*

Start word: thank

Word list: tank, rank, rink, think, pink, punk, funk, dunk, bunk, bonk, honk

Vocabulary practice: rank, rink

Dictation

Write the following words in Elkonin boxes. Remember that glued sounds should stay together in one box since they make a distinct sound when paired.

1. bonk

2. rink

3. gunk

4. plank

Write the following words on the word lines. The ‾GS‾ and ∿ symbols will be located under the word line to remind students to include the glued sound and digraph respectively.

1. flunk

2. wink

3. chunk

Write the following sentences on the sentence lines.

1. Can you fill in the blanks?

2. Honk at the pink pigs to get them off the path!

Glued Sound -nk: Decodable

Read the story. On the back of this sheet, compare Skink and Skunk. How are they different? How are they the same?

Tricky Words: like, to, the, her, of, one, day, he, your, you, she, see, are, make, more, go, to, no

Skink and Skunk

Skink and Skunk are best buds. Skink and Skunk like to snack on bugs. Skink and Skunk like to drink milk. Skink likes to dust and mop her hut, but Skunk likes his hut full of junk. Skink will not go to Skunk's hut. It stinks. Skunk will go to Skink's hut,

but he will bring junk. Skink gets mad when Skunk brings junk. She has to dust and mop a lot more, but she will not tell Skunk that it makes her mad.

One day, Skunk has A LOT of junk! Skink gets mad at Skunk, "I can not stand your junk, Skunk!"

Skunk is sad. He wishes to not make Skink mad. He thinks junk is fun!

"I will help you dust and mop," he tells Skink. Skunk dusts and mops all day. The next day, he sees Skink at her hut. He has no junk, but has bugs and milk!

Name: _____ Date: _____

Glued Sound -nk: Dictation

Elkonin Boxes

1. ▢▢

2. ▢▢

3. ▢▢

4. ▢▢▢

Words   Score: ___ /3 words

1. _____ GS

2. _____ GS

3. _____ GS

Sentences   Score: ___ /17 words

1. _____

2. _____

Word Sort

Cut out the words. Then sort them under the appropriate header.

-ink	*-ank*	*-onk*	*-unk*	chunk	crank
hunk	sink	bonk	shrink	tank	honk
skink	lank	slink	mink	gunk	trunk

Unit 3: Closed Syllables

Types of Syllables

In the *Teach Reading with Orton-Gillingham* curriculum, students will learn six types of syllables. This unit covers closed syllables.

TYPES OF SYLLABLES

	Single Syllable	Multisyllabic
Closed	pan, snack, shrimp	**cat**/**nip**, **in**/**dex**, **rab**/**bit**
Silent *e*	cake, time, stone	**pine**/**cone**, sun/**shine**
Vowel Team/ Diphthong	beach, boat, tree, trout, spoil, taught	**rai**/sin, **pea**/nut, with/**out**, **Au**/gust
Open	why, be	**bo**/nus, **mu**/sic, **ba**/by
***r*-influenced**	fern, hurt, bird	spi/**der**, **twirl**/ing
Consonant -*le*	None	a/**ble**, trem/**ble**

Using Elkonin Boxes with Closed Syllables

At this point in the book, many students are ready to start moving away from Elkonin boxes for individual phonemes and are instead ready to start thinking about words by syllable. We recommend encouraging students to practice this skill during this unit. If they need more practice within individual phonemes, they may choose to break the syllables into smaller parts.

bath	tub

an	them

Closed-Syllable Exceptions

We teach the patterns *ost*, *old*, *olt*, *ind*, and *ild* as glued patterns. When an *i* or *o* begins these patterns, the vowel is long. Therefore, we teach students to place these glued sounds into one box.

ch	ild

Syllabication Rules

Here is a list of syllabication rules to help you as you teach students this concept. Closed syllabication is covered by rules 1 through 5.

1. All syllables have one vowel sound.

2. Compound words should be divided between the two base words.

3. If two consonants appear in between two vowels, divide them in half.

4. If three consonants appear between two vowels, determine which two belong together. Blends and digraphs should not be separated.

5. When one consonant is in between two vowels, first try dividing after the consonant to keep the vowel closed in. If that doesn't sound right, try dividing before the consonant to keep the vowel open.

6. Never divide a vowel team or diphthong in half.

7. If there are two vowels in the middle of a multisyllabic word that do not work as a team, divide them in half.

8. The syllable type consonant *-le* pattern is its own syllable and should be divided as one.

Spelling Rules Covered in this Unit

Closed-Syllable Exceptions: If a word has the pattern *-old*, *-ost*, *-olt*, *-ind*, or *-ild*, the vowel is long.

Exceptions: -ost and *-ind* can be short or long, such as in the words *cost*, *lost*, and *wind*.

The 1•1•1 Rule: If a one-syllable word ends in one vowel followed by one consonant, you must double the consonant when adding a vowel suffix such as in *-ing*, *-ed*, or *-est*.

Exceptions: Do not double the consonant in words ending with *-w*, *-x*, or *-y*, such as in *taxed*, *flowing*, and *staying*.

Which sight words that are not yet decodable should my students know before starting this unit?

the	we	he	have	what	there
be	by	was	make	from	been
look	no	one	down	who	many
said	of	two	how	her	
you	day	like	or	for	
go	my	see	may	your	
so	to	first	out	are	
do	she	come	more	use	

Which new and not-yet-decodable sight words will my students see during this unit?

each	find	way	time	oil
made	now	part	would	these
were	some	they	about	

What other information should I know?

We recommend having your student(s) read the decodable passage before the dictation practice. Also, in some lessons, the Word Sort activity is below the dictation page. We suggest cutting off that section before completing the dictation practice, as some of the words are duplicated.

Lesson 1 | Compound Words

Tips, Tricks, and Details

- Remind students that compound words are words that can stand alone, but when combined, they make a new word.
- Use cocktail straws, playdough, or Wikki Stix to model separating compound words into syllables.

PA Warm-Up

Phoneme Deletion of Initial Sounds

Say the words below. Have students tell you each word without the initial sound.

class (lass)	band (and)	blast (last)
mitt (it)	glad (lad)	cramp (ramp)
clamp (lamp)	mall (all)	mad (ad)
plate (late)	stick (tick)	lap (ap)

Word Work

You will need the following letter tiles for this Word Work activity: *e, n, d, l, e, ss, s, h, p, u, a, b*

This Word Work will require students to change syllables rather than tiles. Each word change will require multiple tile changes.

Start word: endless

Word list: <u>helpless</u>, <u>unless</u>, sunless, <u>hapless</u>, <u>bedless</u>, <u>handless</u>, <u>planless</u>

Vocabulary practice: Suffix: *-less* (without)

Word Sort Possible Words: sunset, catfish, catnip, blacktop, sandbox, offset, sunlit, fishpond, backup, backdrop, eggshell, sunup, backlit, upend

Dictation

Write the following words in Elkonin boxes. **During this activity, encourage students to segment the compound words rather than segmenting by individual phoneme. If needed, students may draw lines within the boxes to segment the words further.**

1. blacktop

2. crosscut

3. fishpond

4. gumball

Write the following words on the word lines. **Symbols for digraphs will no longer be added to the word lines.**

1. fishnet

2. inkwell

3. pickup

Write the following sentences on the sentence lines.

1. It smells like mothballs in granddad's shed.

2. You must bring the eggshells to the bin.

Compound Words: Decodable

Decodable Reader's Theater

Roles: Ann, Link, Narrator

Tricky Words: to, there, are, no, my, said, so, you, the, day, by, was, she, come, me, one

The Catfish Bet

Narrator: Ann and Link wish to fish at Sunset Pond at sunup.

Ann: I wish to catch a catfish!

Link: There are no catfish at Sunset Pond.

Ann: Yes, there are! My grandpop said so!

Link: I bet you six bucks there are no catfish!

Ann: You are on! When I win, I will spend it at the pinball shop.

Narrator: At sunup the next day, Ann and Link sit on the grass by the pond and cast the rods. There is a tug on Ann's rod.

Ann: I got one! I got a...a...shellfish?

Link: Yup! You got a clam!

Narrator: Ann was upset. She sits and sits, and still no catfish. Sunset has come and Link packs up his rod and backpack.

Ann: There is a tug! Help me pull, Link! It is big!

Link: It is! I think you got...a catfish!

Narrator: Ann and Link pull in the catfish. It is a big one!

Ann: I win the bet!

Comprehension

How do you think Link felt when Ann won the bet?

Compound Words: Dictation

Elkonin Boxes

1. [box | box]   3. [box | box]

2. [box | box]   4. [box | box]

Words   Score: /3 words

1. _____   2. _____   3. _____

Sentences   Score: /15 words

1. _____

2. _____

Word Sort

Cut out the words. Then match them with other words to make compound words.

sun	set	cat	fish	egg
nip	black	top	up	shell
sand	box	off	lit	
end	pond	back	drop	

Lesson 2 | Closed Syllables VCCV & VCCCV

Tips, Tricks, and Details

- To facilitate reading and spelling, students should be familiar with syllabication rules. If two consonants appear between two vowels, divide them in half. (cac/tus)
- If three consonants appear between two vowels, determine which two consonants stay together. Blends and digraphs should not be separated. (an/them)

PA Warm-Up

Phoneme Deletion of Initial Sounds

Say the words below. Have students say each word without the initial sound.

finch (inch)	stop (top)	pram (ram)
slap (lap)	pitch (itch)	nor (or)
sleek (leek)	grasp (rasp)	plaid (lad)
hear (ear)	track (rack)	

Word Work

You will need the following letter tiles for this Word Work activity: *sh, i, p, s, m, e, n, t, c, o, m, f, g*

Start word: shipment

Word list: comment, figment, pigment, segment

Vocabulary practice: Suffix: *-ment* (act of doing something, result of action)

Word Sort Possible Words: plastic, address, sudden, griffin, bobbin, humpback, dentist, velvet, pretzel

Dictation

Write the following words in Elkonin boxes. During this activity, encourage students to segment by syllable rather than segmenting by individual phoneme. If needed, students may draw lines within the boxes to segment the words further.

1. combat

2. admit

3. hundred

4. progress

Write the following words on the word lines. Symbols for digraphs will no longer be added to the word lines.

1. until

2. children

3. district

Write the following sentences on the sentence lines.

1. The infant will rest in the basket.

2. Look at the ostrich run in the grassland!

Closed Syllables VCCV & VCCCV: Decodable

Cut out the following sentences and glue them to another sheet of paper in the correct order. Or, number the sentences in the correct order.

Tricky Words: to, have, he, no, how, first, you, of, the, for, go, do, see, she, her, said, down, more

Next, he sets off to the shop to get the snacks. He gets muffins, a big sandwich, plums, chips, and milk.

Montez wishes to have a picnic brunch with his best buds, but he has a small problem. Montez has no snacks, no blanket, and no basket! "How can I have a picnic?" he asks himself.

Montez sets up the picnic. His buds sit down and munch on the snacks. "Yum," Shannon tells Montez, "you must have more picnics!"

The last thing is to call his bud, Shannon, to see if she can bring her quilt and basket. "Yes! I can do that," she tells him.

First, Montez lists the things he must get for the picnic.

Closed Syllables VCCV/VCCCV: Dictation

Elkonin Boxes

1. [|]   3. [|]

2. [|]   4. [|]

Words   Score: /3 words

1. _____   2. _____   3. _____

Sentences   Score: /15 words

1. _____

2. _____

Word Sort (VCCV/VCCCV)

Cut out the syllables. Then match them with other syllables to make two-syllable words.

plas	tic	ad	dress	pret
sud	den	grif	fin	zel
bob	bin	hump	back	
den	tist	vel	vet	

Lesson 3 | Closed Syllables VC/V

Tips, Tricks, and Details

- In Unit 1, students learned that two-syllable words ending with the /k/ sound may end in *c* (panic, comic, topic). This is the first time they will see these words within their reading, so they may need a refresher on this rule.

- In most words with a VCV break in the middle of two syllables, the vowel is long and is separated as V/CV (hotel). In this lesson, the words all have a short vowel with a VC/V split (lemon).

- It is considered a VC/V split if there is a digraph in the middle with a short vowel (method).

- Students will encounter several words with an unstressed syllable, or schwa, sound. This means that the vowel makes a "lazy sound" like a short /ŭ/ because it is unstressed. It is represented by ə.

PA Warm-Up

Phoneme Deletion of Final Sounds

Say the words below. Have students say each word without the final sound.

finch (fin)	beach (bee)	carp (car)
catch (cat)	past (pass)	stalled (stall)
camp (cam)	gasp (gas)	trade (tray)
plate (play)	tricked (trick)	slats (slat)

Word Work

You will need the following letter tiles for this Word Work activity: *i, c, o, m, t, p, a, n, e, l, r*

Start word: topic

Word list: antic, panic, manic, relic, comet, compel

Vocabulary practice: Suffix: *-ic* (having the character or form of; Prefix: *com* (with or together)

Word Sort Possible Words: radish, static, status, satin, robin, rapid, solid, visit, punish, rabid, panic, British

Dictation

> Write the following words in Elkonin boxes. Encourage students to segment by syllable rather than by individual phoneme. If needed, students may draw lines within the boxes to segment the words further.

1. punish   **3.** pocket

2. credit   **4.** topic

> Write the following words on the word lines.

1. rapid   **3.** profit

2. banish

> Write the following sentences on the sentence lines.

1. Bring the wagon down to the cabin.   **2.** I will put the travel bags in the closet.

Closed Syllables VC/V: Silly Decodable

Choose the word you would like to fill in the blank. After you are done selecting your words, reread the story with your selections. Then go back and highlight any words you see that have a VC/V pattern.

Tricky Words: day, be, time, for, the, some, way, to, see, out, they, he, of, go, two, one

The Comic

In six days, it will be time for the talent contest on campus. Some

will travel a long way to see the acts. Janet and Kevin will help

with the talent contest. Janet will help sell tickets and pass out

_____ (wagons/snacks/falcons). Kevin will pass

out _____ (lemon/salad/cactus) drinks.

They will help the comic, Robin, set up his set. He has a lot of props!

Robin is bringing _____ (two/seven/one

hundred) puppets, a rabbit, and a pumpkin for his act.

It is time for Robin to go on. Janet and Kevin yell and clap at

his act. Robin's act is a hit! He wins the contest and gets a

_____ (medal/cabin/dragon).

Comprehension

1. How do Janet and Kevin help with the talent contest?

Closed Syllables VC/V: Dictation

Elkonin Boxes

1. | | |
   |---|---|

2. | | |
   |---|---|

3. | | |
   |---|---|

4. | | |
   |---|---|

Words   Score: /3 words

1. _____   2. _____   3. _____

Sentences   Score: /16 words

1. _____

2. _____

Word Sort

| Cut out the syllables. Then match them with other syllables to create words. Some cards have more than one match. |

rad	ish	stat	ic	pan
sat	in	rob	us	Brit
rap	sol	vis	it	
pun	ish	rab	id	

Lesson 4 | Closed-Syllable Exceptions

Tips, Tricks, and Details

- If a word has the pattern -old, -ost, -olt, -ind, or -ild, the vowel is long.

  Exceptions: -ost and -ind can be short or long as in the words cost, lost, and wind.

- For many students, this is the first introduction to long vowels. We suggest reviewing short vowel sounds prior to teaching the long /ī/ as in wild, and long /ō/ as in most that are covered in this lesson.

- Long vowels are marked with a macron (/ā/ in ape). Short vowels are marked with a breve (/ă/ in apple).

PA Warm-Up

Phoneme Deletion of Final Sounds

Say the words on the list below. Have students say each word without the final sound. Example: mold (mole)

colt (coal)	mild (mile)	wind (whine)
wild (while)	molt (mole)	hold (hole)
fold (foal)	gold (goal)	mind (mine)
bolt (bowl)	told (toll)	sold (soul)

Word Work

You will need the following tiles for this Word Work activity: *olt, old, ost, ind, ild, h, c, m, ch, w, f, k*

Start word: holt

Word list: hold, cold, colt, molt, most, mold, mild, child, wild, wind (long *i*), find, kind

Vocabulary practice: molt, mild, colt

Dictation

> Write the following words in Elkonin boxes. Remember that closed-syllable exception patterns are taught as glued sounds and should be put in one box (see page 101 for details).

1. post
2. wild

3. sold
4. blind

> Write the following words on the word lines. The ‾‾GS‾‾ symbol will be located under the word line to remind students to include the glued sound.

1. holt
2. gold

3. grind

> Write the following sentences on the sentence lines.

1. That wild colt rubs his neck on the post.

2. The kind child will fold the pants for his mom.

Closed-Syllable Exceptions: Decodable

Decodable Comic Strip

Read and illustrate what's happening in the story.

Tricky Words: the, for, she, to, look, by, no, of, see

Rabbit is on the hunt for the best snack. She wishes to find a snack she has not had yet.	Rabbit looks by the gold post. No snacks in that spot!

Rabbit looks by the wild colt's ranch. No snacks in that spot! Then, all of a sudden, Rabbit sees the most vivid thing!	A patch of wild, golden radishes! Rabbit snacks and snacks. Yum!

Name: _____ Date: _____

Closed-Syllable Exceptions: Dictation

Elkonin Boxes

1.

2.

3.

4.

Words   Score: /3 words

1. _____   2. _____   3. _____
         GS   GS   GS

Sentences   Score: /19 words

1. _____

2. _____

Word Sort

Cut out the words. Then sort them under the appropriate header.

Long **O** (*ost, old, olt*)	Long **I** (*ild, ind*)		
told	jolt	host	find
bind	mind	holt	post
child	bold	mild	bolt
wild	sold	most	kind

Spelling Rule | 1•1•1 Rule

Tips, Tricks, and Details

- The 1•1•1 Rule: If a one-syllable word ends in one vowel followed by one consonant, you must double the consonant when adding a vowel suffix.

  - Common Vowel Suffixes: *-ing, -er, -est, -es, -able, -ed, -y, -en*

  Exceptions: Do not double the consonant in words ending with *-w, -x,* or *-y,* such as in taxed, flowy, and staying.

- Prior to spelling words with a suffix, it may be helpful to encourage students to identify and spell the base word.

PA Warm-Up

Phoneme Deletion of Final Sounds (Suffixes)

Tell students you are going to try something new for your PA Warm-Up. Say the words below. Have students say each word without the suffix. For example, if you say "bigger," they say "big." If you say "moldable," they say "mold."

smallest (small)	folded (fold)	letting (let)
changeable (change)	molting (molt)	stopper (stop)
scary (scare)	teacher (teach)	lighten (light)
hopeful (hope)	maddest (mad)	branches (branch)

Word Work

You will need the following letter tiles for this Word Work activity: *-ing, t, r, i, p, p, a, d, d, e, n, s, o, m*

Start word: trip

Word list: tripping, ripping, rapping, rap, rad, red, <u>redden</u>, <u>reddest</u>, <u>red</u>, rod, mod, mop, <u>mopping</u>

Vocabulary practice: Suffixes: *en* (made of, nature of), *est* (most), *ing* (present tense)

Dictation

Write the following words in Elkonin boxes. During this activity, encourage students to segment by syllable rather than segmenting by individual phoneme. If needed, students may draw lines within the boxes to segment the words further. These words follow the VC/CV split (hop/ping).

1. spinning   **3.** matted

2. dampen   **4.** wettest

Write the following words on the word lines.

1. flatten   **3.** smallest

2. jogging

Write the following sentences on the sentence lines.

1. The dog is sniffing the biggest bug on that plant!   **2.** The child is sitting, not picking up the messes.

Spelling Rule 1·1·1 Rule: Dictation

Elkonin Boxes

1. [|]

2. [|]

3. [|]

4. [|]

Words   Score: /3 words

1. _____   2. _____   3. _____

Sentences   Score: /19 words

1. _____

2. _____

Word Sort

Cut out the words. Then sort them under the appropriate header.

Base Word	Consonant Doubles	Consonant Stays the Same	munches
run	kicking	landed	flat
land	fast	running	flatten
jump	fastest	jumping	munch
kick	shop	shopping	

Unit 4: Silent *e*

Jobs of Silent *e*

Silent *e* is most often thought of as a letter at the end of a word that makes the vowel long. While this is the most common job of silent *e*, savvy students may also notice that silent *e* takes on other roles as well. This unit will cover the first two roles of silent *e*.

1. Silent *e* makes the vowel in a word long. This is most often seen in words with one consonant between the vowel and silent *e* (shake, mine, pole).
2. Words in English do not end with *u* or *v*. Words rarely end in an *i* or *z*. Silent *e* is used at the ends of these words (give, blue, tie, freeze).
3. Silent *e* is used at the ends of some words with a *c* or *g* to soften the sounds (hinge, arrange, mice).
4. Silent *e* is used to show that a word is not plural (pulse, lapse).
5. Silent *e* adds a vowel to consonant -*le* syllables (rattle, cable).
6. Silent *e* changes the sound of -*th* to be voiced (clothe, bathe).

Using Elkonin Boxes with Silent *e*

Similar to finger tapping, silent *e* does not get its own Elkonin box since it does not make a sound. Instead, we recommend placing it in the box with the preceding consonant.

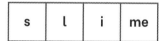

s	l	i	me

Spelling Rules Covered in this Unit

The -*ive* Exception: When a word ends in -*ive*, the vowel can be short or long. This is because words in English cannot end with *v*. A few examples include "give," "chive," "expensive," and "live."

The *e*-Drop Rule: When a word ends in silent *e*, drop the *e* before adding a vowel suffix such as -*ing*, -*ed*, -*er*, or -*est*. Keep it if the suffix begins with a consonant such as -*ly*, -*ment*, or -*ty*.

Exceptions: The *e* is not dropped in words ending with *ee*, *oe*, or *ye* as in "seeing," "hoed," or "dyeing."

It is also not dropped in the words acreage, mileage, and singeing.

Which sight words that are not yet decodable should my students know before starting this unit?

the	day	have	for	way
be	my	make	your	part
look	to	down	are	they
said	she	how	use	time
you	he	or	there	would
go	was	may	been	about
so	one	out	many	oil
do	two	more	each	these
we	like	what	made	
by	see	from	were	
no	first	who	now	
of	come	her	some	

Which new, not-yet-decodable sight words will my students see during this unit?

could	their	new
into	water	sound
other	number	only
word	people	little
write	over	work

What other information should I know?

We recommend having your student(s) read the decodable passage before the dictation practice. Also, in some lessons, the Word Sort activity is below the dictation page. We suggest cutting off that section before completing the dictation practice, as some of the words are duplicated.

Lesson 1 | Magic *e*: *aCe*

Tips, Tricks, and Details

- There are a few words with two consonants between the long *a* and the silent *e* (waste, haste, bathe). You may choose to cover these now, or as they come up. As always, students should try the most common spelling/decoding pattern first and then work through other options as needed.

PA Warm-Up

Phoneme Substitution

Say the words. Have students change one sound in each word with a different letter. For example, say, "Replace the first sound in *chick* with /k/." (kick)

Replace the /p/ in *pail* with /t/. (tail)

Replace the /g/ in *gate* with /l/. (late)

Replace the /j/ in *jar* with /c/. (car)

Replace the /sh/ in *shake* with /b/. (bake)

Replace the /ch/ in *chin* with /k/. (kin)

Replace the /d/ in *ding* with /r/. (ring)

Replace the /s/ in *slick* with /f/. (flick)

Replace the /th/ in *thick* with /p/. (pick)

Replace the /pl/ in *plate* with /g/. (gate)

Replace the /b/ in *bind* with /f/. (find)

Replace the /f/ in *fall* with /c/. (call)

Replace the /st/ in *stone* with /gr/. (groan)

Replace the /sl/ in *slate* with /st/. (state)

Word Work

Instruct the students to begin with the start word. Then go through the list in order by instructing students to build each word with their letter tiles. Students will change one or two tiles at a time. Refer to page 150 for our letter tiles or for tiles in color, visit our website (www.treetopseducation.com/teach-reading). Nonsense words will be marked with a star, and words that require two tile changes will be underlined.

You will need the following letter tiles for this Word Work activity: *e, m, a, t, g, p, c, l, n, an**

Start word: mat

Word list: mate, gate, gape, gap, cap, cape, came, lame, lane, plane, plan, man

**Students should only use the glued -an when forming the words plan and man.*

Vocabulary practice: gape, lame

Dictation

Write the following words in Elkonin boxes. Remember that digraphs and glued sounds stay in one box. The magic *e* should be written in the same box as the preceding consonant since it does not make its own sound.

1. vase

2. stake (The tomato plants were held up by garden stakes.)

3. plate

4. shame

Write the following words on the word lines. The ☆ will be located under the word line to remind students to include the silent *e*.

1. state

2. kale

3. mane

Write the following sentences on the sentence lines.

1. Jane gave the snakes the snack.

2. Save the date for the plane landing.

Magic *e*: *aCe*: Decodable

Decodable Reader's Theater

Roles: Kate, Jake, Narrator

Tricky Words: the, by, we, look, for, to, of, see, you, into, are, down

Snake at the Cave

Kane: The sun is hot! Let's take a snack and hang in the shade by the cave.

Jake: Yes! We can look for snakes and bats.

Narrator: The buds run to the base of the cave.

Kane: It is so hot! Quick! Let's sit in the shade!

Jake: Yes, let's take a rest in the shade to snack on the grapes.

Narrator: The buds sit and snack on grapes when Jake sees that Kane looks pale.

Kane: Is that...a snake?!

Jake: Ahhh! The snake is on you, Kane!

Narrator: Kane jumps up to shake the snake off. The kids run into the cave.

Kane: That was a big snake.

Jake: I am glad we are safe in this cave.

Narrator: Just then, a bat zips down off of the cave wall.

Kane and Jake: AHHHH! Run!

Comprehension

Why do the buds go to the cave? What scares them at the cave? What do you think happens next?

Magic *e*: *aCe*: Dictation

Elkonin Boxes

1.

3.

2.

4.

Words   Score: /3 words

1. _____ ☆   2. _____ ☆   3. _____ ☆

Sentences   Score: /13 words

1. _____

2. _____

Word Sort

Cut out the words. Then sort them under the appropriate header.

a_e	/ă/	rate	rat
snake	snack	rack	rake
gap	gape	fad	fade
whack	wake	cap	cape
sham	shame		

Lesson 2 | Magic *e*: *iCe* & *oCe*

PA Warm-Up

Phoneme Substitution: Consonant Changes

Say the words below, but have students change one sound with a different letter. For example, say, "Replace the first sound in *back* with /p/." (pack)

Replace the /k/ in *kale* with /t/. (tale)

Replace the /m/ in *mate* with /k/. (Kate)

Replace the /j/ in *jam* with /s/. (Sam)

Replace the /th/ in *thumb* with /m/. (mum)

Replace the /ch/ in *choke* with /s/. (soak)

Replace the /d/ in *dire* with /f/. (fire)

Replace the /sh/ in *shire* with /b/. (buyer)

Replace the /th/ in *thirst* with /w/. (worst)

Replace the /dr/ in *drive* with /h/. (hive)

Replace the /bl/ in *bland* with /f/. (fanned)

Replace the /pr/ in *prowl* with /sc/. (scowl)

Replace the /st/ in *stop* with /pl/. (plop)

Replace the /shr/ in *shrink* with /p/. (pink)

Word Work

You will need the following letter tiles for this Word Work activity: *e, i, o, r, p, h, c, n, t, w*

Start word: rip

Word list: ripe, rope, hope, hop, cop, cope, cone, tone, tine, twine, twin, tin

Vocabulary practice: cope, tine, twine

Dictation

> Write the following words in Elkonin boxes. Remember that digraphs and glued sounds stay in one box. The magic *e* should be written in the same box as the preceding consonant since it does not form its own sound.

1. like

2. pole

3. shine

4. quote

> Write the following words on the word lines. The ☆ will be located under the word line to remind students to include the silent *e*.

1. file

2. stone

3. stripe

> Write the following sentences on the sentence lines.

1. The child will win a prize in the bike contest.

2. Can you ride home to get the note?

Magic *e*: *iCe* & *oCe*: Decodable

Read and underline the iCe and oCe words.

Tricky Words: the, are, to, he, they, was, one, day, be, want, go, of, could, see, for, look, there

The Ride of a Lifetime

Miles is a small skink and his home is in the wild. The red skinks in the

thicket are big and not kind to Miles. They like to joke with him and call him

names. They tell him it is all in fun, but Miles thinks it is unkind. One day,

the vile skinks came up with a plan. They put the snack that Miles likes the

most on the end of a kite's rope. They hid by a rock with the kite end. The

vile skinks held on to the rope until Miles came to take a bite of the snack.

They wanted Miles to lift off with the kite. The next day, Miles spotted the

snack. *Sniff, sniff!* "Yum!" Miles did take a bite. Just then, the vile red skinks

let go of the rope. Miles rose up, up, up! He could see all of the globe! He

rode the kite for a while and then the kite's glide came to a stop, on top of

a pine. He looks to the west with a big smile! There are small skinks, just

like him, for miles and miles! This will be Miles's home!

Comprehension

What was the big skinks' joke? Did Miles like the joke?

Name: _____   Date: _____

Magic *e*: *iCe* & *oCe*: Dictation

Elkonin Boxes

1. [| |]   3. [| |]

2. [| |]   4. [| |]

Words   Score: /3 words

1. _____ 2. _____ 3. _____
          ☆   ☆   ☆

Sentences   Score: /18 words

1. _____.

2. _____

Word Sort

Cut out the words. Then sort them under the appropriate header.

i_e	o_e	/ĭ/	/ŏ/
stripe	ship	stole	plod
doll	white	hole	twist
bone	pine	fin	pond
dot	joke	whim	whine

Lesson 3 | Magic *e*: *eCe* & *uCe*

Tips, Tricks, and Details

- Long *u* in a *uCe* can make two sounds. These sounds are /ū/ as in mule and /oo/ as in rude.

- The spelling pattern *eCe* is rare in one-syllable words. It is more common in two-syllable words (delete, complete, extreme).

PA Warm-Up

Phoneme Substitution: Consonant Changes, Initial Sound

Say the words, but have students change the sound with a different letter. For example, say, "Replace the first sound in *share* with /m/." (mare)

Replace the /d/ in *dote* with /t/. (tote)

Replace the /s/ in *style* with /p/. (pile)

Replace the /b/ in *bean* with /s/. (seen)

Replace the /ch/ in *choke* with /p/. (poke)

Replace the /sl/ in *slip* with /tr/. (trip)

Replace the /h/ in *here* with /f/. (fear)

Replace the /sh/ in *sheep* with /b/. (beep)

Replace the /th/ in *there* with /w/. (where)

Replace the /tr/ in *trout* with /p/. (pout)

Replace the /bl/ in *blow* with /fl/. (flow)

Replace the /pl/ in *plunk* with /d/. (dunk)

Replace the /st/ in *stake* with /fl/. (flake)

Replace the /thr/ in *throw* with /m/. (mow)

Word Work

You will need the following letter tiles for this Word Work activity: *e, u, e, th, s, m, n, t, d, d, c, r*

Start word: these

Word list: theme, them, then, ten, <u>tune</u>, dune, dude, <u>crude</u>, rude

Vocabulary practice: dune, crude

Dictation

> Write the following words in Elkonin boxes. Remember that digraphs and glued sounds stay in one box. The magic *e* should be written in the same box as the preceding consonant since it does not form its own sound.

1. mule

2. here

3. plume

4. flute

> Write the following words on the word lines. The ☆ will be located under the word line to remind students to include the silent *e*.

1. mere

2. crude

3. duke

> Write the following sentences on the sentence lines.

1. Is that child cute or rude?

2. Let's mute the TV and play a tune on the flute.

Name: _____   Date: _____

Magic *e*: *eCe* and *uCe*: Dictation

Elkonin Boxes

1. [| |]

2. [|]

3. [| | |]

4. [| |]

Words   Score: /3 words

1. _____ 2. _____ 3. _____
              ☆   ☆   ☆

Sentences   Score: /17 words

1. _____

2. _____

Word Sort

Cut out the words. Then sort them under the appropriate header.

u_e /ū/	u_e /oo/	e_e	theme	cure
dude	fume	fuse	eve	tube
use	dune	rule	plume	muse
cube	here	puke	prune	fluke

Lesson 4 | Multisyllabic Silent *e*

Tips, Tricks, and Details

- When dividing words with syllables that contain a silent *e*, the silent *e* must stay with the vowel it is influencing. Here are some examples of syllable divisions with a silent *e*: case/ment, camp/fire, in/vite.
- The *e*-drop rule will be covered in the next lesson.

PA Warm-Up

Phoneme Substitution: Consonant Changes, Initial Sound

Say the words below, but have students change one sound with a different letter. For example, say, "Replace the first sound in *poke* with /s/." (soak)

Replace the /b/ in *bale* with /m/. (male)

Replace the /t/ in *tile* with /m/. (mile)

Replace the /b/ in *bike* with /m/. (Mike)

Replace the /sh/ in *shake* with /st/. (stake)

Replace the /sh/ in *shine* with /l/. (line)

Replace the /d/ in *dear* with /l/. (leer)

Replace the /cr/ in *crime* with /p/. (pine)

Replace the /sl/ in *slice* with /v/. (vice)

Replace the /t/ in *tote* with /d/. (dote)

Replace the /fl/ in *flame* with /f/. (fame)

Replace the /pl/ in *plate* with /st/. (state)

Replace the /m/ in *make* with /s/. (sake)

Replace the /thr/ in *thrice* with /tw/. (twice)

Word Work

You will need the following tiles for this activity: *c, a, s, ss, e, e, m, n, t, b, l, l, i, i, o, f, ff*

This activity will require students to change one syllable at a time. There are two start words.

Start word: casement

Word list: basement, baseline, offline

Start word: baseless

Word list: toneless, lifeless, lifeline

Vocabulary practice: Suffix: *-less* (meaning without); baseless

Dictation

Write the following words in Elkonin boxes. Remember that digraphs and glued sounds stay in one box.

1. complete

2. explode

Write the following words on the word lines. The ☆ will be located under the word line to remind students to include the silent *e*.

1. convene

2. extreme

3. capsize

Write the following sentences on the sentence lines.

1. Let's invite Steve to the bash by the flagpole.

2. Helene will play the trombone, but she dislikes the song.

Multisyllabic Silent *e*: Decodable

Decodable Comic Strip

Read, then illustrate what's happening in the comic.

Tricky Words: was, he, the, would, to, one, day, could, first, of, they, said, now

James was an athlete. He was the best at baseball.	He would wake up at sunrise to run drills. He would swing the bat, run the bases, and pitch and catch the balls.

One day, James broke his leg while running the bases. He was upset he could not compete at the big game and he did not wish to miss it.	James had a plan! He could be an umpire! First, he had to check with all of the athletes. They all said, "Yes!" Now James can be in the big game!

Multisyllabic Silent *e*: Dictation

Elkonin Boxes

Words   Score: ___ /3 words

1. _____   2. _____   3. _____
         ☆   ☆   ☆

Sentences   Score: ___ /19 words

1. _____

2. _____

Word Sort

Use the syllables to make real words. Some syllables have more than one pair.

com	plete	back	stroke	en
pire	um	vam	con	grave
clude	ex	hale	in	sun
vite	wild	life	line	shine

Spelling Rule | *-ive* Exception

Tips, Tricks, and Details

- *-ive* exception: When a word ends in *-ive*, the vowel can be long or short.
- This exception is taught because of the spelling rule pertaining to the letters *v, j, i,* and *u.* There are no English words that end in *v* or *j,* and very few that end in *i* or *u.* Because of this, words that end with a /v/ sound are followed by an *e.*
- Words that do end in these letters are either abbreviations (flu, deli) or words that are foreign (tofu, ravioli).

PA Warm-Up

Phoneme Substitution: Consonant Changes, Final Sound

Say the words below, but have students change one sound with a different letter. For example, say, "Replace the last sound in *plane* with /t/." (plate)

Replace the /k/ in *make* with /d/. (made)

Replace the /b/ in *probe* with /z/. (prose)

Replace the /s/ in *base* with /t/. (bait)

Replace the /z/ in *faze* with /t/. (fate)

Replace the /m/ in *fame* with /k/. (fake)

Replace the /l/ in *stale* with /t/. (state)

Replace the /z/ in *doze* with /t/. (dote)

Replace the /v/ in *pave* with /d/. (paid)

Replace the /d/ in *made* with /l/. (male)

Replace the /n/ in *tine* with /m/. (time)

Replace the /st/ in *waste* with /d/. (wade)

Replace the /sp/ in *wasp* with /sh/. (wash)

Replace the /mp/ in *lump* with /k/. (luck)

Word Work

You will need the following letter tiles for this Word Work activity: *d, r, i, v, e, h, ch, g, l, f, j*

Start word: drive

Word list: dive, hive, chive, give, live*, five, jive

Vocabulary practice: hive, jive

*You may choose to pronounce this with a long *i* or short *i.*

Dictation

> **Write the following words on the word lines.**

1. active

2. outlive

3. captive

> **Write the following sentences on the sentence lines.**

1. Is that buzzing from the massive hive up there?

2. Let's drive to see the festive homes.

Spelling Rule: *-ive* Exception: Decodable and Dictation

Tricky Words: to, the, for, first, you

Fill in the Blank

chives	give	olives	dive

1. You can _____ Pete the fins for his

_____.

2. First, bake the chicken, then you add the _____

and _____.

Words   Score: /3 Words

1. _____   2. _____   3. _____

Sentences   Score: /16 words

1. _____

2. _____

Word Sort (-ive exception)

Cut out the words. Then sort them under the appropriate header.

Short *i*	Long *i*	give	olive	chive
active	drive	strive	thrive	hive
offensive	pensive	forgive	live	
five	dive	effective	attentive	

Spelling Rule | e-Drop Rule

Tips, Tricks, and Details

- e-Drop Rule: When a word ends in silent *e*, drop the *e* before adding a vowel suffix such as *-ing*, *-ed*, *-er*, and *-est*. Keep the *e* if the suffix begins with a consonant such as *ly*, *ment*, or *ty*. Like any rule, there are a few exceptions.
  - Words ending with a soft *c* or *g* followed by an *e* and *-able* do not drop the *e* (*changeable, noticeable*).
  - Words ending with *-ee*, *-oe*, *-ye* do not drop the *e* (*fleeing, canoeing, dyeing*).

PA Warm-Up

Phoneme Substitution: Consonant Changes, Final Sound

Say the words below, but have students change one sound with a different letter. For example, say, "Replace the last sound in *crane* with /z/." (craze)

Replace the /v/ in *pave* with /d/. (paid)

Replace the /b/ in *lobe* with /d/. (load)

Replace the /m/ in *dime* with /v/. (dive)

Replace the /z/ in *daze* with /t/. (date)

Replace the /m/ in *home* with /l/. (hole)

Replace the /l/ in *mole* with /t/. (moat)

Replace the /p/ in *gape* with /t/. (gate)

Replace the /t/ in *flute* with /m/. (flume)

Replace the /d/ in *grade* with /n/. (grain)

Replace the /n/ in *tone* with /t/. (tote)

Replace the /st/ in *haste* with /l/. (hail)

Replace the /ct/ in *tact* with /k/. (tack)

Replace the /mp/ in *limp* with /st/. (list)

Word Work

You will need the following letter tiles and syllable tiles for this Word Work activity: *h, o, p, e, m, r, i, s, d, -ing, t*

Start word: hope

Word list: hoping, moping, roping, rope, ripe, <u>ripest</u>, <u>ripe</u>, rise, rising, riding, ride

Vocabulary practice: moping, ripe

Dictation

Write the following words on the word lines.

1. waded

2. liking

3. basement

Write the following sentences on the sentence lines.

1. The kids go skating on the frozen pond.

2. I am hoping he is inside baking the cake for us.

Name: _____   Date: _____

e-Drop: Decodable and Dictation

Tricky Words: we, go, down, the, for, so

1. We can go (slideing/sliding/slidding) down the hill.

2. Mike (saved/saveed/savved) the snack for the cute dog.

3. "Hold on, I am (mutting/muteing/muting) the TV so we can chat."

Words   Score: /3 Words

1. _____   2. _____   3. _____

Sentences   Score: /19 words

1. _____

2. _____

Word Sort

Cut out the words. Then sort them under the appropriate header.

No *e*-Drop	*e*-Drop	liking	pavement	dyeing
statement	ripen	cutest	hiding	making
toning	hopeless	useful	latest	
casement	timing	baking	hateful	

Unit 5: Vowel Teams

What is a regular vowel team?

A regular vowel team is a predictable set of two vowels that generally follow the rule "when two vowels go walking, the first one does the talking." This phrase is only true about 40 percent of the time, so teachers should explain to students that they will learn many other vowel patterns that do not follow this logic.

How can I help my student identify which vowel team to use during dictation?

Vowel teams can often be generalized by the location in which they appear in words. There are exceptions to these patterns, but here is what you can teach your student to expect when reading and spelling words with predictable vowel teams:

Where are these vowel teams most commonly found?

Vowel Team	Beginning	Middle	End
ea	x	x	x
ee	x	x	x
ai	x	x	
ay			x
oa	x	x	
oe			x
ue		x	x
ui		x	
ie (ī)			x

Which sight words that are not yet decodable should my students know before starting this unit?

the	of	come	for	part	number
be	day	have	your	they	people
look	my	down	are	would	over
said	to	how	there	about	new
you	she	or	been	oil	sound
go	he	may	many	could	only
so	was	out	each	other	little
do	one	what	were	word	work
we	two	from	now	write	know
by	see	who	some	their	
no	first	her	way	water	

Which new, not-yet-decodable sight words will my students see during this unit?

place	after	great
year	our	where
me	good	
very	sentence	

What are homophones?

Homophones are words that sound the same but have different meanings and/or spellings. Words like *sea/see*, *tail/tale*, and *road/rode* are fun for students to find in text. Homophones will appear frequently during this unit.

What other information should I know?

We recommend having your student(s) read the decodable passage before the dictation practice. Also, in some lessons, the Word Sort activity is below the dictation page. We suggest cutting off that section before completing the dictation practice, as some of the words are duplicated.

Lesson 1 | Vowel Teams *ee* & *ea*

Tips, Tricks, and Details

- The *ea* and *ee* spelling do not have a clear spelling rule. One generalization is that *ee* is often used in nature (tree, sheep, beet, bee, etc.) and *ea* words are often "wet" or "dinner" words (beach, stream, sea, treat, feast, meal, meat).

- The most common sound of *ea* is a long /ē/, as taught in this lesson. However, the *ea* pattern can also sound like short /ĕ/ (bread, wealth) and long /ā/ (steak, great).

PA Warm-Up

Phoneme Substitution: Vowel Changes

Say the words below, but have students change the vowel sound with a different vowel sound. For example, say, "Replace the /ē/ in *team* with /ā/." (tame)

Replace the /ā/ in *tail* with /ī/. (tile)

Replace the /ā/ in *play* with /ē/. (plea)

Replace the /ē/ in *treat* with /ī/. (trite)

Replace the /ē/ in *seem* with /ā/. (same)

Replace the /ō/ in *groan* with /ā/. (grain)

Replace the /ū/ in *cue* with /ā/. (cay)

Replace the /ī/ in *tie* with /oo/. (too)

Replace the /ō/ in *doe* with /ā/. (day)

Replace the /ā/ in *trace* with /ŭ/. (truss)

Replace the /ē/ in *these* with /ō/. (those)

Replace the /ū/ in *mute* with /ā/. (mate)

Replace the /ō/ in *tone* with /ī/. (tine)

Replace the /ī/ in *tile* with /ē/. (teal)

Word Work

Instruct the students to begin with the start word. Then go through the list in order by instructing students to build each word with their letter tiles. Students will change one or two tiles at a time. Refer to page 150 for our letter tiles or for tiles in color, visit our website (www.treetopseducation.com/teach-reading). Nonsense words will be marked with a star, and words that require two tile changes will be underlined.

You will need the following letter tiles for this Word Work activity: *ea, ee, s, w, p, l, m, d*

Homophones: (sea-see, seam-seem)

Start word: sweep

Word list: sleep, seep, see, sea, seal, seam, seem, seed, seep, deep, deem

Vocabulary practice: seep, deem

Dictation

Write the following words in Elkonin boxes. Remember that digraphs, glued sounds, and vowel teams stay together in one box.

1. creep

2. lead

3. teach

4. beech (The beech tree provided shade for the picnic.)

Write the following words on the word lines. The $\overline{VT}$ symbol will be located under the word line to remind students to include the vowel team.

1. peach

2. feast

3. coffee

Write the following sentences on the sentence lines.

1. That wild beast has big teeth!

2. Shall we go to the beach or the creek?

Vowel Teams *ee* & *ea*: Decodable

Partner Poem
Tricky Words: the, go, to, my, we, are, our, become, from, of, do, out, day

The Sea of Dreams

Reader 1:

I will go to the sea
With my bud, Bea
We will collect green glass from the shore.

Reader 2:

The bucket we hold
Has shells, glass, and gold
The beach is not a bore.

Reader 1:

The waves appear teal
As we eat a hot meal
And peek at the waves a bit more.

Reader 2:

We share things from our weeks
And sit on seats made of teak
We chat about the things that are in store.

Readers 1 and 2:

We watch the waves crash
Our minds do not dash
As we share our dreams out in the sand
The water is teal, our dreams will become real, as we chat that day at the shore.

Comprehension

What do the friends do at the beach?

What does the line, "We chat about the things that are in store," mean?

Vowel Teams *ee* & *ea*: Dictation

Elkonin Boxes

1.
<table>
<tr><td></td><td></td><td></td><td></td></tr>
</table>

3.
<table>
<tr><td></td><td></td><td></td></tr>
</table>

2.
<table>
<tr><td></td><td></td><td></td></tr>
</table>

4.
<table>
<tr><td></td><td></td><td></td></tr>
</table>

Words   Score: /3 words

1. _____   2. _____   3. _____
           VT   VT   VT

Sentences   Score: /15 words

1. _____

2. _____

Word Sort

Cut out the words. Then sort them under the appropriate header.

ea	*ee*	meal	reel	zeal
real	teeth	beam	seed	steam
bead	street	cream	beep	
steep	queen	preach	cheat	

Lesson 2 | Vowel Teams *ai* & *ay*

Tips, Tricks, and Details

- The *ai* spelling is used in the beginning and middle of words. The *ay* spelling is used at the end of words.

PA Warm-Up

Phoneme Substitution: Vowel Changes

Say the word on the list, but have students change one sound with a different letter. For example, say, "Replace the /ĭ/ sound in *chick* with /ŭ/." (chuck)

Replace the /ā/ in *fail* with /ō/. (foal)

Replace the /ā/ in *say* with /ō/. (sew)

Replace the /ē/ in *team* with /ī/. (time)

Replace the /ē/ in *tree* with /ā/. (tray)

Replace the /ō/ in *boat* with /ă/. (bat)

Replace the /oo/ in *blue* with /ō/. (blow)

Replace the /ī/ in *pie* with /ā/. (pay)

Replace the /ō/ in *toe* with /ē/. (tea/tee)

Replace the /ā/ in *bake* with /ŭ/. (buck)

Replace the /ū/ in *mule* with /ā/. (male)

Replace the /ō/ in *dote* with /ā/. (date)

Replace the /ī/ in *time* with /ĭ/. (Tim)

Word Work

You will need the following letter tiles for this Word Work activity: *ea, ai, ay, s, t, r, l, m, f, b*

Start word: stray

Word list: stay, ray, tray, ray, say, sea, seal, sail, tail, trail, rail, frail, fail, mail, may, bay

Vocabulary Practice: frail, bay

Dictation

Write the following words in Elkonin boxes. Remember that digraphs, glued sounds, and vowel teams stay together in one box.

1. fray

2. brain

Write the following words on the word lines. The $\overline{\text{VT}}$ symbol will be located under the word line to remind students to include the vowel team.

1. rail

2. bray

3. strain

Write the following sentences on the sentence lines.

1. Will the snail in that pail miss the sea?

2. The gray cat is old and frail.

Name: _____ Date: _____

Vowel Teams *ai* & *ay*: Silly Decodable

Choose the word you would like and then fill in the blank. After you are done selecting your words, read the story with your selections. Then go back and highlight any words you see that have an *ai* or *ay* vowel team pattern.

Tricky Words: the, out, from, says, come, would, he, to, now, of

The Stray

Is that _____ (dog/snail/goblin) a stray on the hiking trail? Jay sees a _____ (black/pink/green) tail with gray spots on it. It is peeking out from a bush. The stray has a chain on its _____ (leg/neck/tail). It is frail and afraid! Jay says, "Come here, I am kind." The stray is wet with _____ (rain/paint/mud). It did _____ (jump/sway/stop) at Jay's feet. Jay can see that the stray would like to _____ (play, sleep, paint). Jay gets the chain off of him. He pets the stray and gets the wet stains off of it. Jay gave the stray a name. The name was _____ (Kail/Kay/Zain). The stray gave him a hug. The stray is not afraid now! The stray is _____ (glad/asleep/eating). Now the stray has a home. He will not need to live on the trail.

Comprehension
Describe the stray animal.

Why do you think the animal was afraid?

Vowel Teams *ai* & *ay*: Dictation

Elkonin Boxes

1. | | | |
|---|---|---|
| | | |

2. | | | | |
|---|---|---|---|
| | | | |

Words   Score: /3 words

1. _____   2. _____   3. _____
        VT   VT   VT

Sentences   Score: /16 words

1. _____

2. _____

Read & Fill in the Blank

Read each word and underline the *ai* or *ay* vowel team.

1. grain   fray   raisin   essay

Fill in the missing vowel team.

2. pl_____n   gr_____   hallw_____   j_____l

Word Sort

Cut out the words and pictures. Then sort them under the appropriate header.

ai	*ay*	sail	ray	stay	play
frail	pray	tail	clay	main	train
braid	gray	stain	may		

Lesson 3 | Vowel Teams *oa* & *oe*

Tips, Tricks, and Details

- The *oa* spelling is used in the beginning and middle of words. The *oe* spelling is used at the end of words.
- The *oe* spelling is a rare spelling pattern. Oftentimes, if the long /ō/ is at the end of a word, it is spelled with *ow* (snow, elbow). See Unit 8 in *Teach Reading with Orton-Gillingham* for more on this pattern.

PA Warm-Up

Phoneme Substitution: Vowel Changes

Say the words below, but have students change the vowel sound with a different sound. For example, say, "Replace the /ā/ in *grail* with /oo/." (gruel)

Replace the / ō/ in *foal* with /ĭ/. (fill)

Replace the /ā/ in *tray* with /ē/. (tree)

Replace the /ē/ in *beam* with /oo/. (boom)

Replace the /ē/ in *street* with /ā/. (straight)

Replace the /ō/ in *groaning* with /ĭ/. (grinning)

Replace the /oo/ in *cruel* with /aw/. (crawl)

Replace the /ī/ in *vie* with /ow/. (vow)

Replace the /ō/ in *hoe* with /ā/. (hay)

Replace the /ā/ in *taking* with /ĭ/. (ticking)

Replace the /ū/ in *future* with /ē/. (feature)

Replace the /ō/ in *motel* with /ŏ/. (mottle)

Replace the /ī/ in *striped* with /ă/. (strapped)

Word Work

You will need the following letter tiles for this Word Work activity: *oa, oe, g, l, t, b, s, c, m, h, d, f*

Start word: gloat

Word list: goat, boat, boast, coast, coat, moat, <u>moe</u>, hoe, doe, foe, <u>foam</u>

Vocabulary Practice: gloat, boast, foe

Dictation

> Write the following **words** in Elkonin boxes. Remember that digraphs, glued sounds, and vowel teams stay together in one box.

1. coal

2. foe

3. roast

4. toe

> Write the following words on the word lines. The $\overline{\text{VT}}$ symbol will be located under the word line to remind students to include the vowel team.

1. hoe

2. groan

3. goals

> Write the following sentences on the sentence lines.

1. The man will groan if you step on his toe.

2. The mole and foal are foes.

Vowel Teams *oa* & *oe*: Decodable

Tricky Words: there, the, around, they, have, her, to, are, out, what, she, would, were

The Home on the Coast

There is a big home on the coast. It has a moat that runs around it. The moat has toads, fish, and a small boat! Inside of the moat is a big, green plot with hundreds of goats. The kids that live near it claim that a witch lives inside. The kids boast that they have seen her casting spells on kids to make them toads. The kids say she eats roach loaf and goats' toes. Joe thinks that is false. His goal is to meet the "witch" and find out what she is like.

Joe and his bud Moe approach the home on the coast. A kind old adult greets them with a smile. She invites the buds in and tells them her name is Roe. She tells them that she has the goats to make goat cheese and goat milk. She sells the goats' milk and cheese as a job. The goats drink from the moat.

Roe gives the buds cheese and tea. She tells them that she is not a witch and would like to meet Joe and Moe's buds to give them the same treats.

The buds leave the home on the coast with a grin. The buds gloat that they were brave and tell the kids that Roe keeps goats, not witch spells!

Comprehension

Why do the kids think the home has a witch inside?

Why does Roe keep goats?

Vowel Teams *oa* & *oe* Dictation

Elkonin Boxes

1. [| |]

3. [| | |]

2. [|]

4. [|]

Words

Score: _____ /3 words

1. _____   2. _____   3. _____
            VT   VT   VT

Sentences

Score: _____ /16 words

1. _____

2. _____

Fill in the Blank

Fill in the missing *oa* or *oe* vowel team.

d_____   thr_____t   upl_____d   tipt_____

Word Sort

Cut out the words. Then sort them under the appropriate header.

oa	*oe*	toad	toe	aloe
float	hoe	soar	Moe	approach
toast	Joe	soap	doe	
gloat	roach	throat	cloak	

Lesson 4 | Vowel Teams *ue, ui, & ie*

Tips, Tricks, and Details

- Long *u* can make two sounds. The most common is /oo/, as in *blue*. It can also sound like /yoo/, as in *hue*.

- The spelling pattern *ui* occurs in the middle of words. The spelling pattern *ue* can be found in the middle or ends of words.

- The *ie* spelling pattern is very uncommon. The long *i* sound at the end of a word is more commonly represented by a *y*.

- Students may need a reminder about the silent *e* in singular words ending in the /s/ sound.

PA Warm-Up

Phoneme Substitution: Vowel Changes

Say the words below, but have students change the vowel sound with a different sound. For example, say, "Replace the /ū/ in *cruise* with /ā/." (craze)

Replace the /ō/ in *oat* with /ā/. (ate)

Replace the /ā/ in *day* with /oo/. (do)

Replace the /ē/ in *meaner* with /ō/. (moaner)

Replace the /ē/ in *greet* with /ā/. (great)

Replace the /ō/ in *groaner* with /ē/. (greener)

Replace the /ū/ in *hue* with /ī/. (hi)

Replace the /ī/ in *pie* with /ā/. (pay)

Replace the /ō/ in *toe* with /ā/. (hay)

Replace the /ā/ in *cable* with /ŏ/. (cobble)

Replace the /ū/ in *tunic* with /ŏ/. (tonic)

Replace the /ō/ in *doting* with /ā/. (dating)

Replace the /ī/ in *binding* with /ŏ/. (bonding)

Word Work

You will need the following letter tiles for this Word Work activity: *f, r, ui, t, s, ue, c, l, d, ie, p*

Start word: fruit

Word list: suit, seat, sue, cue, clue, due, die, pie

Vocabulary practice: sue, cue

Dictation

Write the following words in Elkonin boxes. Remember that digraphs, glued sounds, and vowel teams stay together in one box.

1. fuel

2. tie

3. blue

4. bruise

Write the following words on the word lines. The $\overline{\text{VT}}$ symbol will be located under the word line to remind students to include the vowel team.

1. value

2. pie

3. cruise

Write the following sentences on the sentence lines.

1. Will she rescue the man in the swimsuit?

2. The pie has blue fruit.

Name: _____ Date: _____

Vowel Teams *ue*, *ui* & *ie*: Silly Decodable

Choose the word you would like to fill in the blank. After you are done selecting your words, reread the story with your selections. Then go back and highlight any words you see that have a *ui*, *ue*, or *ie* vowel team pattern.

Tricky Words: first, to, she, the, from, there, no, for, her, are, we, so, into

The Fruit Pie

Gran makes the best fruit pies! The pies are sweet, blue, and best hot from the oven. Gran spends a whole day to make them.

First, Gran gets a pan, whisk, and _____ (squids/red fruit/glue). Next, she collects the blue fruit from the _____ (tree/bush/blue cave beast). She must run to get it so she will not run into _____ (Sue/the cave beast/the fruit criminal). She likes to chat and there is no time for that!

The fruit will stain her hands and top, so she must put on a blue _____ (suit/tee/dueling vest) to keep her clothes clean. Then, she will crush the _____ (fruit/crust/melon). It gives her hands a dull hue. Last, she will put the pie in the oven to bake. When it is complete, we will all eat it! _____ (Yum/Yuck)!

Comprehension

What makes Gran's pie so good?

How does Gran bake her pie?

Vowel Teams *ue*, *ui* & *ie*: Dictation

Elkonin Boxes

1. [| |]

2. [|]

3. [| |]

4. [| | |]

Words   Score: /3 words

1. _____   2. _____   3. _____
           VT   VT   VT

Sentences   Score: /13 words

1. _____

2. _____

Word Sort

Cut out the words. Then sort them under the appropriate header.

ue	*ui*	*ie*	rescue	cue
fruit	pie	blue	cruise	hue
die	fuel	bruise	tie	
subdue	suitcase	cruel	recruit	

See page 12 for information regarding the use of these tiles.

a	e	e	i	o	u	ai	ay
ea	ee	oa	oe	ie	ue	ui	
b	c	d	f	g	h	j	k
l	m	n	p	qu	r	s	s
t	v	w	x	y	z	ch	tch
ck	sh	th	wh	ff	ll	ss	zz
all	am	an	ank	ink	onk	unk	olt
ost	old	ang	ing	ung	ind	ild	ive

ABOUT THE AUTHORS

Heather MacLeod-Vidal is a former teacher, tutor, educational business owner, and coauthor of *Teach Reading with Orton-Gillingham*. She works as a literacy specialist to support students with dyslexia and other learning differences in a Tampa Bay area school. She has a degree in elementary education from the University of Tampa and is endorsed in reading, ESOL, and exceptional student education. Passionate about teaching all children to read, Heather is currently pursuing a masters in special education with a focus on dyslexia at the University of Florida. She lives in Gulfport, Florida, with her husband, two children, and a variety of rescue animals.

Kristina Smith received a bachelor of arts degree in sociology from the University of South Florida. Upon graduating, she began her teaching career with Hillsborough County Public Schools, where she taught pre-kindergarten to fifth-grade students with various learning disabilities. Continuing to pursue her love of helping children, she attended Florida State University where she received her Master of Social Work degree. For two years, Kristina provided therapy to children with emotional and mental health disorders before she narrowed her focus back to children with learning differences. Since 2014, she has trained in Orton-Gillingham, taught numerous students who struggle with reading and math, and has coauthored a curriculum for teachers who wish to help their struggling students with reading. Kristina is still an educator and resides in Panama City Beach, Florida, with her husband.

To learn more about Heather and Kristina's resources for struggling readers, please visit their website, www.treetopseducation.com, or search Treetops Educational Interventions on Teachers Pay Teachers.